"LORD, TEACH US TO PRAY," Jesus' disciples asked. And he taught them. Not only words to pray ("Our Father") but about being a prayer: "Every one who asks receives," which literally is "Every asker receives."

This is what I like about *"Pray For Me"*: My friend Ken Carter provides a Bible study, a theological reflection, a practical guide to prayer, and more. He helps us to see prayer as essentially what we most deeply are—intercessors. Every breath, every thought, every act directed toward God on behalf of others is prayer. So read this, and be one of Christ's pray-ers.

—Leighton Ford
President, Leighton Ford Ministries
Charlotte, North Carolina

— Kenneth H. Carter Jr. —

"Pray *for* me"

The Power in Praying
for Others

UPPER
ROOM BOOKS®
NASHVILLE

Cover design: MTW Design / www.mtwdesign.net
Cover image: www.ThinkStock.com
Interior design: PerfecType, Nashville, TN

Library of Congress Cataloging in Publication
"Pray for me" : the power of praying for others / Kenneth H. Carter, Jr.
      p. cm.
  Includes bibliographical references (p.   ).
  ISBN 978-0-8358-1090-6
  1. Intercessory prayer—Christianity. I. Title.
  BV215.C366 2012
  248.3'2—dc23   2011044201
  ISBN 978-0-8358-1020-6

For ordinary Christians,
men and women,
laity and clergy,
who take the ministry of intercession seriously,
and for my spiritual mentors and
teachers along the way.

Contents

The Empty Bucket

"PRAY FOR ME"

For twenty-eight years I have been a pastor in local congregations. Besides the recurring pattern of the Christian year, celebrations of Christmas and Easter, weddings, memorial services, visitation of the sick, and confirmation classes, the request for intercessory prayer is a constant.

On the way out of a service, an elderly man will say quietly, "Please pray for my wife"; an e-mail message arrives: "Please pray for my sister who lives in another state." Or the request may be more direct: "Pray for me. I have a real challenge ahead."

I have always responded that I would pray. But in reality, and in hindsight, my actual response was at times perfunctory: a fleeting thought or just writing down a name on a page, to give to others later. The motivation to write this book came in part from what seemed my own pastoral failure—I was being asked for spiritual help and attention, but I was not giving the request the engagement it merited.

Even more troubling was the knowledge that many expect the ordained—those set apart—to have the expertise and the time to provide this spiritual support. Intercessory prayer is not exclusive to ordained persons—we share intercession with all of God's people, and you may be reading this book because you are a gifted intercessor or feel called to pray for others. But it was this concern as a pastor that prompted me to take intercession more seriously.

Here I will share some of what I have learned so that you may be more prepared when someone says to you, "Pray for me."

THE BUCKET

The words *Pray for me* signal a person in need. And when someone is in need—because of illness, a broken relationship, loss of work, a spiritual crisis, or grief, it is as if he or she is carrying a heavy bucket—a bucket filled with emotion, filled with grief, filled with confusion, filled with disappointment.

I learned about the bucket image from a pastor friend. We come from different denominations but share an interest in equipping people to care for one another and to draw nearer to God in retreat settings. This powerful image of the bucket has elucidated intercessory prayer for me.

A person in need or in grief is carrying around this bucket of emotion. An *intercessor* is one who comes alongside that individual with an empty bucket. The person in need gives his or her agenda to the intercessor, and the intercessor receives that agenda as the work of God, namely prayer. Intercession is carried out by those with enough space in their lives to include the needs of others: family, friends, congregations, communities, and the world.

EMPTYING OURSELVES

Let the same mind be in you that was in Christ Jesus,
 who, though he was in the form of God,
  did not regard equality with God
  as something to be exploited,
 but emptied himself,

taking the form of a slave,
being born in human likeness.
And being found in human form,
he humbled himself
and became obedient to the point of death—
even death on a cross.—Philippians 2:5-8

Intercessors follow the example of Jesus, and we need to consider the cost of having the mind that was in Christ Jesus. Intercession requires emptying oneself on behalf of another.

When we worship, we move into the presence of a Holy God. We offer gifts of praise and silence, listening and humility, adoration and repentance. We place these gifts upon the altar. We gaze upon the greatest act of intercession, the cross of Jesus Christ. And we remember that Jesus continues to pray for us. He is the great high priest, seated at the right hand of God.

To make intercession is to worship God. All along the way, we are praising the God who hears our prayers, who is "our help in ages past, our hope for years to come." We "lay aside every weight and the sin that clings so closely" (Heb. 12:1). We empty ourselves. We look to Jesus, who emptied himself, who endured the cross, who is seated at the right hand of the throne of God (Heb. 12:2).

As you read these pages, as you journey more deeply into a life of intercession, imagine that you are a part of a great procession approaching the throne of grace. You are not alone. You are laying your burdens before the altar. You are preparing for something. Perhaps you are preparing for a more profound ministry of intercession.

I have learned to honor the request "pray for me." It is a cry for help, however it may be expressed. It is an acknowledgment that we are limited and finite creatures. It is a trust placed in a higher power. It is always prompted by a situation that would not be desired: an illness, a loss, a need, a crisis, a doubt—and yet it is always an occasion for the grace of God, whose power is made perfect in our weakness (2 Cor. 12:9).

That intersection—God's power and our weakness—lies at the heart of intercession. May the grace of God lead you into a deepened life of prayer for others.

Chapter One

Intercession and Scripture
Old Testament

I f we are to pray for others, we need to know the traditions, teachings, and practices of intercession found in scripture. These are God's design for authentic intercession. They will guard us from errors of judgment and motivate us to continue in prayer, especially when we are tempted to give up. Chapters 1 and 2 focus on particular models of intercession from the scriptures, first from the Old Testament, and then from the New Testament. Biblical teaching undergirds this whole study, but these two chapters provide a foundation.

It will be helpful to have an open Bible nearby as we learn more about intercession. First we turn to the Torah, the Prophets, and the Wisdom Literature. We will focus on Moses, Elijah, and the psalmist.

MOSES AS INTERCESSOR

When the people saw that Moses delayed to come down from the mountain, the people gathered around Aaron, and said to him, "Come, make gods for us, who shall go before us; as for this Moses, the man who brought us up out of the land of

Egypt, we do not know what has become of him." Aaron said to them, "Take off the gold rings that are on the ears of your wives, your sons, and your daughters, and bring them to me." So all the people took off the gold rings from their ears, and brought them to Aaron. He took the gold from them, formed it in a mold, and cast an image of a calf; and they said, "These are your gods, O Israel, who brought you up out of the land of Egypt!" When Aaron saw this, he built an altar before it; and Aaron made proclamation and said, "Tomorrow shall be a festival to the LORD." They rose early the next day, and offered burnt offerings and brought sacrifices of well-being; and the people sat down to eat and drink, and rose up to revel.

The LORD said to Moses, "Go down at once! Your people, whom you brought up out of the land of Egypt, have acted perversely; they have been quick to turn aside from the way that I commanded them; they have cast for themselves an image of a calf, and have worshiped it and sacrificed to it, and said, 'These are your gods, O Israel, who brought you up out of the land of Egypt!'" The LORD said to Moses, "I have seen this people, how stiff-necked they are. Now let me alone, so that my wrath may burn hot against them and I may consume them; and of you I will make a great nation."

But Moses implored the LORD his God, and said, "O LORD, why does your wrath burn hot against your people, whom you brought out of the land of Egypt with great power and with a mighty hand? Why should the Egyptians say, 'It was with evil intent that he brought them out to kill them in the mountains and to consume them from the face of the earth'? Turn from your fierce wrath; change your mind and do not bring disaster on your people. Remember Abraham, Isaac, and Israel, your servants, how you swore to them by your own self, saying to them, 'I will multiply your descendants like the stars of heaven, and all this land that I have promised I will give to your descendants, and they shall inherit it forever.'" And the LORD changed his mind about the disaster that he planned to bring on his people.—Exodus 32:1-14

A biblical understanding of intercession surely begins with the example of someone like Moses, whom, according to the Torah, "the LORD knew face to face" (Deut. 34:10). Moses is set apart from the beginning of his life—saved in a basket (literally an ark) that floats down the river; called aside by the Voice from within the burning bush, commissioned as the one who will speak to Pharaoh the oppressor. Throughout the book of Exodus, God speaks to Moses, guiding him, correcting him, encouraging him, at times with words—"I will be with you"—at other times with visible signs—plagues, cloud, fire, and manna.

In Exodus, Mount Sinai is a holy place (Exod. 19:23). There God gives Moses the commandments (Exod. 20). Later, at the end of Moses' life, God is with him on another mountain, Mount Nebo. God points to the Promised Land, allowing Moses to see it, but letting him know that Moses will not be allowed to enter it. In the Gospels, Jesus is transfigured on a "high mountain" (Matt. 17:1-2). Moses appears there, along with Elijah.

Invitation to reflect: Mountain peaks are holy places throughout the scriptures. Recall what you would consider a mountaintop experience in your own life or a geographical mountain setting that is important to you. How has that experience or place affected your faith journey?

Moses has been on the mountain for forty days and forty nights. Moses is the leader of the people, but in his absence there is a void in leadership. So the people make demands on the logical person who is present: Aaron. They demand: "Come, make gods for us, who shall go before us"; the idea of "going before" is also present in Exodus 13 (a cloud by day, a fire by night). Their true leader, Moses, is almost forgotten ("as for this Moses, the man who brought us up out of the land of Egypt, we do not know what has become of him"). In contemporary parlance, they might have asked, "Moses, what have you done for us lately?"

We have short memories. When God is absent, we look for substitutes. My neighbor Steve Shoemaker has written: "When times get hard and God seems nowhere to be found, the consolations of what we can see and touch, taste and smell are awfully appealing: the feel of gold, the taste of skin, the smell of the soil, the sea. Golden calves often beat out the impalpable God."[1]

And so the Hebrew people demand other gods. Aaron, their leader, is either overwhelmed with doubts or intimidated, or perhaps some combination of both. In the end, he gives in to the demands of the people.

Invitation to reflect: Think about your own sphere of influence. Can you relate to Aaron's predicament? Recall an instance when you've been tempted to give people not what they need but what they desire.

The people take the gold rings from their ears and bring them to Aaron. Aaron melts the gold and casts an image of a calf. They said, "These are your gods, O Israel, who brought you up out of the land of Egypt!" (Exod. 32:4), in clear violation of the second commandment. Human beings are worshiping creatures; when we refuse to worship the One God, we bow down to worship many gods (Rom. 1).

Seeing all this, the Lord sends Moses back down the mountain at once to the scene of the idolatry and unfaithfulness. The people are indicted. Israel is no longer "my people" but "*your* people" (Exod. 32:7, emphasis added). God mediates and intervenes through people like Moses—and perhaps you and me. Next comes a curious development in the story. The Lord says, "Now let me alone, so that my wrath may burn hot against them and I may consume them;

and of you I will make a great nation" (32:10). Is God brooding? Does God need solitude? The rabbis who reflected on this story thought so. But a period of solitude and reflection gives Moses the time to consider his own action as well. What should Moses do?

He *intercedes*. "Moses implored the LORD his God, and said, 'O LORD, why does your wrath burn hot against your people, whom you brought out of the land of Egypt with great power and with a mighty hand?" (32:11). Moses speaks on behalf of his people. Here Moses fulfills the role of priest. Moses speaks boldly to God, and there is give and take in this relationship. Moses reminds God that these are "your people"! He reminds God of the divine reputation: "Why should the Egyptians say, 'It was with evil intent that he brought them out to kill them in the mountains, and to consume them from the face of the earth'? Turn from your fierce wrath."

Moses says to the Lord, don't you remember who you are? You are "the Lord [who is] . . . merciful and gracious, *slow to anger,* and abounding in steadfast love" (Exod. 34:6, emphasis added). Moses pleads with God: "Change your mind and do not bring disaster on your people" (Exod. 32:12).

The persistence of Moses leads to theological questions: Can or should we expect God's mind to be changed? Moses does not let up! "Remember Abraham, Isaac, and Israel, your servants, how you swore to them by your own self, saying to them, "I will multiply your descendants like the stars of heaven, and all this land that I have promised I will give to your descendants, and they shall inherit it forever'" (Exod. 32:13).

Moses appeals to the nature of God, which is to keep faith with promise and covenant. Moses knew the history and character of God. He knew the frailty and error of his own people. And yet Moses refused to allow the relationship to end. And finally, "the LORD changed his mind about the disaster that he planned to bring on his people" (Exod. 32:14).

Invitation to reflect: We sometimes imagine that God is unchanging, and yet there are clearly alterations or shifts in God's discernment and thinking here. What does this say to you about the nature of God? Do you find the thought of a God whose mind can be changed to be encouraging or uncomfortable?

THE INTERCESSIONS OF THE PROPHETS

Then Elijah said to the people, "I, even I only, am left a prophet of the LORD; but Baal's prophets number four hundred and fifty."—1 Kings 18:22

[The angel of the Lord] said, "Go out and stand on the mountain before the LORD, for the LORD is about to pass by." Now there was a great wind, so strong that it was splitting mountains and breaking rocks in pieces before the LORD, but the LORD was not in the wind; and after the wind an earthquake, but the LORD was not in the earthquake; and after the earthquake a fire, but the LORD was not in the fire; and after the fire a sound of sheer silence. When Elijah heard it, he wrapped his face in his mantle and went out and stood at the entrance of the cave. Then there came a voice to him that said, "What are you doing here, Elijah?" He answered, "I have been very zealous for the LORD, the God of hosts; for the Israelites have forsaken your covenant, thrown down your altars, and killed your prophets with the sword. I alone am left, and they are seeking my life, to take it away." Then the LORD said to him, "Go, return on your way to the wilderness of Damascus; when you arrive, you shall anoint Hazael as king over Aram. Also you shall anoint Jehu son of Nimshi as king over Israel; and you shall anoint Elisha son of Shaphat of Abel-meholah as prophet in your place. Whoever escapes from the sword of Hazael, Jehu shall kill; and whoever escapes from the sword of Jehu, Elisha shall kill. Yet I will leave seven thousand in Israel, all the knees that have not bowed to Baal, and every mouth that has not kissed him."
—1 Kings 19:11-18

Do you ever sense that God is speaking through you? Are you puzzled, challenged, or even angered by what is going on in the world? Do you wonder why there seems to be such a huge gap between the world that God intended and the way things are? Do you ever find yourself asking God to intervene in events, to change the course of history, to bring about peace and justice and righteousness?

In the Bible, prophets are those who speak God's word into a present situation. They are in tune with the events of their time—warfare, poverty, worship of false gods, complacency—and they also are open to the will of God. "Everyone more or less believes in God," Eugene Peterson has written. "But most of us do our best to keep God on the margins of our lives, or, failing that, we refashion God to suit our convenience. Prophets insist that God is the sovereign center, not off in the wings awaiting our beck and call. And prophets insist that we deal with God as God reveals himself, not as we imagine him to be."[2]

The perception that prophets predict the future is only partially true. Prophets are given a vision that has implications for the present and the future. At times the work of the prophet can be lonely, as Elijah confessed to the Lord.

Invitation to reflect: When have you felt that you were praying for an outcome that seemed unlikely, and that you were in the minority in making your appeal to God?

We can think of intercession as priestly work—speaking to God on behalf of the people, speaking to people on behalf of God—but intercession is also a prophetic ministry. In the Hebrew Bible, the books written by the prophets are the second major portion of scripture, following the Law. Prophets like Isaiah, Jeremiah, and Ezekiel called the people to follow God's law, to remember God's salvation, to accept God's judgment, and to receive God's mercy. They did this by making the word of God plain ("thus says the LORD") and by pointing others to signs. Jeremiah spoke of a potter working with clay, which communicated that God is free to shape and mold us for a variety of purposes. Ezekiel envisioned a valley of dry bones, reminding us that God can bring life out of death.

Elijah is often regarded as representative of all of the prophets. His story in 1 Kings narrates the struggle between the worship of God in contrast to the worship of Baal. Overtaken by fatigue and fear, Elijah complains to God. God listens, and God reminds Elijah that he is not alone. Elijah is sent forth: "Go, return on your way to the wilderness" (1 Kings 19:15). God overlooks Elijah's tendency to cast blame on Israel. Like so many of us, Elijah overestimates the obstacles before him. God keeps Elijah's focus on the future and upon the vision that will be fulfilled.

The prophetic words are always vivid and stark. They get our attention! The prophets spoke chiefly against two evils: (1) the tendency to worship other gods, and (2) neglect of the poor. They challenge the complacent and self-sufficient, warning them of coming disaster. They comfort the people in exile, driven from their homes, assuring them of protection. In their own time, and today, the prophets envision a reality so different from what we know that we are forced to look and listen. In a vision of the "Peaceable Kingdom," Isaiah spoke of the wolf living with the lamb. In a world marked by war, violence, and conflict, the prophets present God's vision for the world and call us to live toward that vision.

Martin Luther King Jr., a prophetic witness in the last century, reminded people of the difference between their public profession ("that all are created equal") and their practice in regard to people of other races. He called Christians to listen to the prophets. He often quoted a favorite scripture from the prophet Amos: "Let justice roll down like waters, and righteousness like an ever-flowing stream" (5:24). In this way King's voice followed in the tradition of the prophets of ancient Israel.

Invitation to reflect: Meditate on the words of Amos 5:24. Say them slowly. Imagine that you are speaking these words to God, as appeal, as demand. Now imagine that the Lord is speaking these words to you, also as appeal and as command.

It has been said that the role of the prophet is to afflict the comfortable and to comfort the afflicted. To those who are comfortable and complacent the prophets bring a warning. To those who are suffering and burdened the prophets bring a word of hope. Who are the prophetic voices in your own community?

Invitation to reflect: What would your community look like if God's vision for it were to become a reality? Who are the comfortable in your community? Who are the afflicted in your community? How can you remember both these groups in your prayers?

INTERCESSION AND THE PSALMS:
JOY OF HUMAN DESIRING

O God, you are my God, I seek you,
    my soul thirsts for you;
my flesh faints for you,
    as in a dry and weary land where there is no water.
So I have looked upon you in the sanctuary,
    beholding your power and glory.
Because your steadfast love is better than life,
    my lips will praise you.
So I will bless you as long as I live;
    I will lift up my hands and call on your name.
My soul is satisfied as with a rich feast,

and my mouth praises you with joyful lips
when I think of you on my bed,
    and meditate on you in the watches of the night;
for you have been my help,
    and in the shadow of your wings I sing for joy.
My soul clings to you;
    your right hand upholds me.

But those who seek to destroy my life
    shall go down into the depths of the earth;
they shall be given over to the power of the sword,
    they shall be prey for jackals.
But the king shall rejoice in God;
    all who swear by him shall exult,
    for the mouths of liars will be stopped.—Psalm 63

To thirst is to long for something essential. The psalmist knew about this longing. Psalm 63 is a psalm of David, the ascription tells us, when David was in the wilderness of Judah.

Do we know what it is like to thirst for something essential in the wilderness? Amid loneliness and isolation many search for community in a variety of ways. I once served a church that included a very fine bass voice among the men, and each summer he would sing the national anthem at the local Minor League Baseball game. It was always wonderful, and many of us came along to enjoy the game and offer moral support. This outing usually occurred on what was known as Thirsty Thursday. If you use your imagination, you can figure out what Thirsty Thursday was all about! Lots of people—very thirsty people—sharing fellowship; at the same time, a baseball game was taking place!

But thirst has a more basic meaning. I opened the newspaper a few months ago to read about a local woman's trip to Bolivia. I have traveled to this beautiful country. She had been, more specifically, to Cochabamba. I've been there as well. Bolivia is landlocked—devoid of harbors and beaches, and water supplies are critically low. The people of Cochabamba were rioting because of lack of water. Very thirsty people.

It is not accidental that the scriptures speak of water in describing our human longings and desirings. My soul thirsts for you, for God, the psalmist writes, in the midst of the wilderness.

Invitation to reflect: Do we know what it means to thirst for God? to want God as much as a man or woman in the midst of the Judean wilderness wants something essential, a drink of water? to want God as much as the people of Cochabamba, who were rioting for water?

To thirst for God is to desire God; it is to know that God is essential. Sometimes we have to be in the wilderness before we recognize our thirst, our desires. The Bible speaks of wilderness as a place of testing, trial, emptiness, absence. The rabbis called the wilderness the school of the soul. In the wilderness we discover the essential.

If you have experienced a serious illness or medical uncertainty, you know about wilderness. If you have experienced any form of prejudice, you know about wilderness. If you have lived in depression, you know about wilderness. If you have felt like you were in the wrong place or have walked in the darkness of grief, you know about wilderness. To be in the wilderness is like being in a dry and weary land without water. In the Christian season of Lent, we see the geography of wilderness in our spiritual lives. Lent is forty days of wilderness, a time of discovering that the temptations of Jesus are our own testings. Lent reminds us that life is difficult, and, further, that Christian life is difficult. There are mountaintops, but there are also valleys. There are rainbows, but there are also storms. There are sunrises, but there are also sunsets. There are Easter mornings, but there are also Good Fridays. There are beautiful spring days, but there is also the dead of winter. Most of us have made this journey. We've been there!

Invitation to reflect: Recall a wilderness experience that called forth your deep prayers, for self and others. When did the experience occur, and what was it like?

Psalm 63 helps us name all of this. John Chrysostom, an early church father, insisted that "no day should pass without singing this Psalm." We plan our lives, we make preparations, we try to control outcomes and events, but some day, some time, somewhere, when we least expect it, we will find ourselves in the wilderness. It helps to know that. A false teaching about Christianity denies this truth, claiming that if we love God, if we follow Jesus, if we serve our neighbor, life will blossom in abundance and overflowing. We discover insights about two realities of life in this psalm: *spiritual dryness* and *spiritual darkness.*

Invitation to reflect: Recall a time when you prayed in the midst of darkness and dryness. What was the experience like? What did you learn about yourself? And what sustained you?

One of the *Screwtape Letters* of C. S. Lewis talks about spiritual dryness. Screwtape, writing to his nephew, who is a devil in training, describes the work of God that goes on in our lives: "In His efforts to get permanent possession of a soul, He relies on the troughs even more than on the peaks; some of His special favourites have gone through longer and deeper troughs than anyone else."[3] This remarkable comment follows not much later in the letter: "The prayers offered in the state of dryness are those which please Him best."[4]

Spiritual dryness implies thirsting for something, desiring something, maybe God. We also may know spiritual *darkness*. The psalms refer repeatedly to this condition:

> I . . . meditate on you in the watches of the night. (Ps. 63:6)
> Surely the darkness shall cover me. (Ps. 139:11)
> In the shadow of your wings I will take refuge, until the destroying storms pass by. (Ps. 57:1)
> Even though I walk through the darkest valley, I fear no evil. (Ps. 23:4)

For most Christians, wilderness is a part of the faith journey. There are times to bask in the sunshine and times to hide in the shadows. Psalm 63 describes the shadow times in life. Many people turn to the Bible, and maybe even to the church, for safety, for security, for refuge. The psalmist writes, "You have been my help, and in the shadow of your wings I sing for joy" (v. 7).

What does it mean to be in the shadow of God's wings? In the darkness, we cannot always see, and yet we trust. In the darkness, we sense the dangers of life, and yet we trust. In the darkness, we sense that death is approaching, and yet we trust: in the words of an old hymn, "Abide with me; fast falls the eventide."

In the Christian tradition this experience has been known as the "dark night of the soul." In the dark night there are no visible signs of God's presence; it may be the pruning we read about in John 15; in the Passion, it is the stripping down of Christ, the emptying that we read about in Philippians 2; in the seasons of the year, it is the cold and snow of winter. The dark night purges all our assumptions, our support systems, all forms of light. We are in the darkness.

And yet, paradoxically, we find ourselves in the shadow of God's wings. There we sing, "Abide with me." In the dark night of the soul, God is preparing us for the light.

We encounter times of spiritual dryness and spiritual darkness throughout our journeys. How do we live, how do we survive, how do we make our way through wilderness times? How do we intercede? One answer is that we are given the desire for something, a desire for something that will quench our thirst, a desire for something that will light our way.

And so we return to the questions *What do we desire the most? What is essential?* Of course, our desires can get all out of focus. We can desire the wrong things; these become compulsions, addictions. Marketers can teach us to desire what that may or may not be helpful to us.

Two simple truths about desires are notable for a Christian. First, *God desires us.* The One who created us also loves us. Augustine said, in a prayer to God, "You have made us for yourself, and our heart is restless until it rests in you."[5] David Ford, a theologian at Cambridge, observes, "If we get the desire for God right, everything else follows."[6] We love, because God first loved us. We desire God, because God has first desired us. We intercede, knowing that God has interceded on our behalf. We yearn for God and find it amazing that God has first yearned for us. Amazing. We need reminders of this truth, or it will get crowded out amid all the other messages we receive. Hymns remind us: it is grace, amazing grace. Scripture remind us: it is God's gift, this life, the life to come, all a gift. Worship reminds us: baptism, a new identity; Communion, a renewed promise to feed us and sustain us, like manna in the wilderness. The wisdom and love of friends remind us, in Sunday school classes and in circles and in small groups, and wherever two or three are gathered in his name: we are the beloved children, and God desires us.

This truth of God's love leads to another. The abundant life consists of *desiring what God desires.* How do we make our way through times of dryness and darkness? We continue to say the prayers, even when we don't feel anything. We continue loving, even when we don't feel worthy of love. We continue to worship, even when it does not please us to worship. We take one step at a time, even when we do not see very far into the future. We do the next thing; we eat the next meal, remembering that the promise is for daily bread and that God sustained the people with manna in the wilderness each day, enough for that day.

Our desires as Christians are always translated into small works, practices, gestures. And so we are led to the water, and we take a drink. We hide in the shadows of God's presence and watch for the morning.

The good news is that when we are ready for something that is essential, God will give it to us. When we were children, we learned to distinguish between what we wanted and what we needed. What we need is water, living water, like the woman, a Samaritan, who discovered Jesus at the well and said, "Give me this water, so that I may never be thirsty" (John 4:15).

Maybe you are reading this and reflecting on it, and you are really thirsty, spiritually dehydrated, emotionally empty. Maybe you are listening, you are in the shadows, you are in the dark night, spiritually lost, emotionally bewildered.

Invitation to reflect: Listen to the good news of the scripture.

If you are in the wilderness of fatigue, hear the good news—"The LORD is my shepherd, I shall not want . . . he leads me beside still waters." (Ps. 23:1-2)

. . . in the wilderness of depression—"With joy you will draw water from the wells of salvation." (Isa. 12:3)

. . . in the wilderness of being alone in your convictions—"You are like a tree planted by streams of water." (Ps. 1:3)

. . . in the wilderness of the deepest valley—"Though I walk through the darkest valley, I fear no evil; for you are with me." (Ps. 23:4)

. . . in the wilderness of grief—"The lamb at the center of the throne will be their shepherd, and he will guide them to springs of the water of life, and God will wipe away every tear from their eyes." (Rev. 7:17)

If you are in the wilderness, God's gift to you is Psalm 63. It is a prayer offered in a state of dryness, in a moment of darkness. It is a prayer that pleases God, the God who enters into your wildernesses, the God who desires you, the God who seeks you and finds you, the God who prays for you.

Invitation to reflect: How might Psalm 63 be a prayer offered for those who do not have the faith or strength to pray it for themselves? Think of someone who is in a place of spiritual dryness or darkness. Consider praying this psalm on behalf of that individual.

These passages of scripture from the Law, the Prophets, and the Psalms remind us of the importance of prayer in the Old Testament. Now we turn to the New Testament, as we deepen our foundation for a life of intercession.

Chapter Two

Intercession and Scripture
New Testament

When they came to the disciples, they saw a great crowd around them, and some scribes arguing with them. When the whole crowd saw him, they were immediately overcome with awe, and they ran forward to greet him. He asked them, "What are you arguing about with them?" Someone from the crowd answered him, "Teacher, I brought you my son; he has a spirit that makes him unable to speak; and whenever it seizes him, it dashes him down; and he foams and grinds his teeth and becomes rigid; and I asked your disciples to cast it out, but they could not do so." He answered them, "You faithless generation, how much longer must I be among you? How much longer must I put up with you? Bring him to me." And they brought the boy to him. When the spirit saw him, immediately it convulsed the boy, and he fell on the ground and rolled about, foaming at the mouth. Jesus asked the father, "How long has this been happening to him?" And he said, "From childhood. It has often cast him into the fire and into the water, to destroy him; but if you are able to do anything, have pity on us and help us." Jesus said to him, "If you are able!—All things can be done for the one who believes." Immediately the father of the child cried out, "I believe; help my unbelief!" When Jesus saw that a crowd came running together, he rebuked the unclean spirit, saying to it, "You spirit that keeps this boy from speaking and hearing, I command you, come out of him, and never enter him again!" After crying out and convulsing him terribly, it came out, and the boy was like a corpse, so that most of them said, "He is dead." But Jesus took him by the hand and lifted him up, and he was able to stand. When he had entered the house, his disciples asked him privately, "Why could we not cast it out?" He said to them, "This kind can come out only through prayer."—Mark 9:14-29

Imagine a large teaching hospital. The masses stream in the doors speaking different languages—Spanish and Arabic and English; they are people of all ages, from the very young to the very old. A young boy is having a hard time; you can hear his teeth grinding, and you can see infection around his mouth; he is seriously ill. Then your eyes meet his mother's eyes; obviously she is also suffering, perhaps from lack of sleep. The mother knocks on the office door of the diagnostician, the professor who really has the gift; his name is legendary in the hospital and outside it.

"Professor, can you take a moment and look at my boy?" Before she is even asked, the mother goes into detail—describing every ailment, every affliction, every medication, every false hope. "I've already seen your students," the mother says, "and they were of no help." She hopes that she has found a *real* doctor.

In the story we read from the Gospel of Mark we find the parallels: a boy is sick; in place of a mother is a father, and the doctor is a rabbi, whose name is Jesus, and the medical students are his disciples. The story relocated to our contemporary context makes so much sense, and yet when we read the healing miracles, like this one, sprinkled throughout the four Gospels, they seem foreign to us. In this passage from Mark, a boy has been afflicted with seizures for some time. The father brings the child to the rabbi. Jesus attends to the child. "Bring him here," he says.

But not before a comment about his students, Jesus' disciples, the "faithless generation." So much has been invested in them, and yet it seems they don't get it; they can't do it. "How are they ever going to become doctors? Everything I teach them," the rabbi laments, "goes in one ear and out the other!"

And so Jesus says, thinking of the boy again, "Bring him here." The father places the boy before Jesus, and here is the first lesson: we must put ourselves in a place where we are likely to meet Jesus. Unless we travel to that teaching hospital, we are never going to be in the presence of the professor. Sometimes healing is up to us. Some part of getting well has to do with our initiative.

Invitation to reflect: Recall a time when you had an insight or came to the decision that you would need to act differently in order to become whole or well.

In that moment when Jesus and the father meet, some kind of battle ensues between Jesus and this spirit that has overtaken the boy. In the Old Testament, Jacob wrestles with an angel (see Gen. 32). In the Gospel story, Jesus wrestles with a demon. It is all going the wrong way. "How long has this been going on?" Jesus asks. "Since he was little," the father responds, "but if you are able to do anything, have compassion on us and help us."

"If you are able!—All things can be done for the one who believes," Jesus responds.

Here we learn a second lesson related to intercession: what seems impossible to us is possible with God. The parameters of our thinking or the limitations of our imagination do not confine God. Who are we to place limits on what God can do?

I created the heavens and the earth, God says.
I created light and darkness, God says.

I breathed life into humanity, and you became a living soul, God says.

I roll away the stone, and command you to rise up and walk, God says.

Invitation to reflect: In your intercession, consider the following questions. Can HIV/AIDS be cured in this world? Can hunger be abolished in this world? Can poverty be eliminated in this world? Can warfare cease and swords be turned into plowshares in this world? Can lost people experience conversion?

Everything is possible to the one who believes. What seems impossible to us is possible with God. The father begs Jesus, "If you are able to do something, help us." When Jesus tells him, "everything is possible to the one who believes," the father responds, "I believe; help my unbelief." Here is a third lesson: all of us have within ourselves a mixture of belief and unbelief. This reality goes against the grain of conventional Christianity, but it is true; it is liberating, even biblical: we all live with this intermingling of belief and unbelief.

Maybe you find yourself in times of prayer reflecting on all that we struggle with on this planet or perhaps a problem closer to home: a family relationship, a financial crisis, a work issue, or conflict with a neighbor. Could it be different? Is there a solution? Maybe you understand where the father is coming from: "I believe; help my unbelief!"

The man speaks honestly with Jesus. He could have simply told him what he thought Jesus wanted to hear: "Sorry, Jesus, I wasn't thinking, of course you can do it all." We think first of deferring to authority. We think doubt is the enemy of faith. But he is honest. If you practice the memorization of scripture, try this one: "I believe; help my unbelief." The struggle between belief and unbelief, faith and doubt, is built into the biblical story. Jacob, wrestling with a powerful, destructive force, says, "I will not let you go, unless you bless me" (Gen. 32:26). Have you ever been in a situation where you thought, *I have been through too much here not to get something good out of this!*

In Mark's story, Jesus heals the boy. The spirit comes out, and the boy becomes very still, like a corpse, Mark says. Most of the students misdiagnose it all, of course: "Looks like he's dead." Jesus must have been saying, "You have already forgotten the important lesson." What seems impossible to us is possible with God.

Jesus then takes the boy's hand and lifts him up, and he stands. It's like a resurrection. This is the good news. Our God heals. Our God gives life. Sometimes the healing comes in this life. And sometimes the healing comes in the resurrection. But that's not the end of the story. The students gather around the professor. They are shaking their heads: *Why can't we do that?*

We watch a pro hit a golf ball, and we say, "Why can't I do that?" We listen to someone in the choir sing a solo, and we say, "Why can't I do that?" We are in the presence of a master chef; the plate arrives, we taste the food, and it is delicious, and we say, "Why can't I do that?" If the father is honest about his lack of faith, the disciples are honest about their limitations. Here is a fourth fundamental lesson for the life of prayer: we can always learn from our failures.

The disciples' question, *Why can't we do that?* is the human question. Have you ever failed at anything? I have. The disciples had failed. Jesus tells them this kind of healing happens only through prayer. A final lesson: where our energies end, God's power begins. You've been trying to do all of this, Jesus reminds the disciples, *without a prayer*. Prayer, it turns out, is the key to it all. Our lack of faith has everything to do with our lack of prayer. Throughout the Gospels we find these alternating rhythms in the life and ministry of Jesus:

- action and prayer,
- engagement and withdrawal,
- ministry and retreat,
- service and silence.

There are days filled with meeting people, someone touching the hem of Jesus' garment and the spirit flowing out of him; other days begin in a lonely place before sunrise. Jesus heals; but make no mistake, Jesus also prays. Perhaps Jesus is reminding the disciples of this pattern. The disciples see the action, the external result, and want to replicate it, but the teacher is reminding them that what happens in the silence, in the stillness, when no one is looking, has everything to do with the healing of the boy.

Why can't we do this? This kind of thing happens only by prayer.

I ponder all of this from the perspective of a pastor. I was ordained twenty-eight years ago. A bishop preached the ordination sermon; to be honest, I cannot remember the bishop's name! I don't remember his name, in the same way that some of us hear high school or college graduation speeches, and a few years later we cannot recall who gave them!

I don't remember who preached, but I do remember one sentence in the sermon: "If you don't pray every day, if you don't have some regular discipline of prayer, you will be out of the ministry in five years."

The teacher was saying to us, the students, that this kind of thing only happens by prayer.

In intercession we go the place where the healing stream flows, to the place where Jesus is. Let us remember that what is impossible for us is possible for God.

Let us be honest enough to say that we all carry around some mixture of faith and doubt. Let us learn from our failures. Let us remember that where our energies end, God's power begins.

And in learning these lessons, let us be a part of healing the broken, repairing the world, redeeming the creation.

For the one who believes, all things are possible.

INTERCESSION IN THE WRITINGS OF PAUL

For all who are led by the Spirit of God are children of God. For you did not receive a spirit of slavery to fall back into fear, but you have received a spirit of adoption. When we cry, "Abba! Father!" it is that very Spirit bearing witness with our spirit that we are children of God, and if children, then heirs, heirs of God and joint heirs with Christ—if, in fact, we suffer with him so that we may also be glorified with him.—Romans 8:14-17

Romans 8 has been called the inner sanctum of the cathedral of the Christian faith. We are standing on holy ground when we read these words: "all who are led by the Spirit of God are children of God" (v. 14). We are no longer slaves, and here the reader remembers Egypt, and Pharaoh, and the oppression of human bondage. We are children of God.

Paul is talking about the new life and the old life, a theme he has been working with since the fifth chapter of Romans. "You did not receive a spirit of slavery to fall back into fear," Paul reminds these new Christians (v. 15). When Moses had led the people out of slavery, he held before them a vision of entering the Promised Land. But on the way they had to pass through the wilderness. The wilderness was chaotic, dangerous, and uncertain. The people were hungry, thirsty, and confused. Some wanted to go back to Pharaoh; "at least in Egypt we had three meals a day," they said.

Jameson Jones, the dean of Duke Divinity School when I was a student, once said that every church he had served had a "Back to Egypt" committee! That's because change is hard, and the future is always unpredictable, and sometimes we know we are on the way to the Promised Land but now it seems like wilderness, and like the country song says, we long for "the good old days when times were bad."

Invitation to reflect: How do you most often reflect on the past? Do you recall both the good and the bad? Do you see events through a nostalgic haze? How does the way you view the past carry forward into the present, particularly as you perceive your own personal situation and events that shape the church, community, nation, or world?

You didn't receive a spirit of slavery to fall back into fear, but you have received a spirit of adoption. Paul invites us to reflect on our identity. We are not God's biological children. We are not Christians because of our race or ethnicity. We have been adopted (Galatians 3). We are not slaves. We are the adopted children of God. Then Paul tells us what it means to be a child of God.

Growing up in the church, I knew instinctively what it meant to be a child of God. I knew it from sitting next to my grandfather and drawing pictures on pieces of paper that he would bring (he didn't want me wasting the church envelopes). And I knew it from a couple of songs that we would sing. Some of our best theology has always been present in our simplest music.

Jesus loves the little children,
All the children of the world.
Red and yellow, black and white,
they are precious in His sight,
Jesus loves the little children of the world.

Jesus loves the children of Haiti and Sudan, Jesus loves the children of Israel and Palestine, Jesus loves the children of Afghanistan and Iraq. Jesus loves the children of the United States. Jesus loves children who are healthy and children who are sick, children who are safe and children who are missing. *All the children of the world . . .* We also sang another song:

> Jesus loves me! This I know, for the Bible tells me so.
> Little ones to him belong; they a re weak, but he is strong.
> Yes, Jesus loves me! Yes, Jesus loves me!
> Yes, Jesus loves me! The Bible tells me so.

These songs taught me that I was a child of God, and that Jesus loved me.

Invitation to reflect: Spend a few moments in the presence of God, to whom you belong as a child. What do you hope to hear? What would you like to say?

In Romans 8 Paul is teaching the early Christians that *they* are children of God. Just as those songs from childhood planted ideas in us, Paul plants two memories through this text: a word and a sign.

Word: *Abba*

The word is *Abba*. When we cry *Abba*, it is the spirit bearing witness with our spirit that we are children of God. *Abba* is the Aramaic word for "father." Aramaic was the language that Jesus spoke. In the garden of Gethsemane, Jesus prayed, "Abba, Father, for you all things are possible; remove this cup from me" (Mark 14:36). The Spirit prompts us to use the same word Jesus used as we address God.

Abba was not a formal word for a cold and distant father figure. The word does not pertain to parental authority. *Abba* was an intimate name for a parent, which might be used only within the household. We are children of One who knows and loves us

37

intimately, and because we are adopted children, we also know that we have been chosen. This is a basic concept of what it means to be a Christian. God's Spirit dwells within us, and we know that we are God's children: "Little ones to him belong."

We are a part of the family. There is a powerful longing to be a part of the family. Think of popular contemporary stories about children raised by aunts and uncles, father figures, and adoptive parents: Luke Skywalker in *Star Wars*; Bilbo and Frodo in *The Lord of the Rings*; Harry Potter. These stories grab people. Folks wait in line to buy the books and see the movies because the stories tap into our powerful longing to belong. We knew it when we were children. We sang it: "Little ones to him belong." "When we cry, 'Abba! Father!' it is that very Spirit bearing witness with our spirit that we are children of God" (Rom. 8:15-16).

Sign: The Cross

If we are children of God, Paul says, we have an inheritance: the future glory, the Promised Land, the life to come. But on the way we are going to struggle. On the way we are going to pass through the wilderness. And that brings us to the second way we know we are children of God: the sign of the cross. We are "heirs of God and joint heirs with Christ—if, in fact, we suffer with him so that we may also be glorified with him" (Rom. 8:17). Paul continues: "I consider that the sufferings of this present time are not worth comparing with the glory about to be revealed to us" (Rom. 8:18). Paul speaks of the suffering of God's children because he wants us to understand that life is not always going to be a playground. We are children of God, but we must also become children of God.

How do we become children of God? Not through biology or genetics. Not by being born into the right family. We become children of God as we discover this relationship with the One whom Jesus called Abba, Father. One of the best ways to discover this relationship is to pray the Lord's Prayer. We also become children of God as we suffer, under the sign of the cross. That concept challenges us, because we want to shield our children from suffering. We ourselves want to avoid suffering. I want to avoid suffering. From time to time, when I visit a dentist, I thank God for the scientist who invented novocaine!

But we live in a world that suffers. Paul uses a clear image: the old world is crumbling—like the stock market in a nosedive. The creation is in decay. But something is about to happen. It's like pregnancy. The whole creation has been groaning in labor pains, and not just the creation, but we ourselves. While my wife could speak from experience on this matter, we can say that in pregnancy life is not the way it used to be, and life is not the way it's going to be.

The pain of labor is bearable because we live in hope; and in hope, Paul says, we are saved. In the meantime, the Christian life may be painful, like labor; messy, like childbirth. The Christian life also could be compared to being adopted into a family; we're not really like the father or the mother, but if we live around them long enough and listen to them attentively enough, we will become more like them.

We live with a word, *Abba*, and a sign, *the cross*, and a hope for what we do not yet see. We await something new, something that will change our lives, something we cannot make happen. How do we know this? The Spirit is with us, the Holy Spirit, a gift we celebrate at Pentecost, the presence of God that resonates with our spirit. "The spirit helps us in our weakness," Paul promises. And then a liberating word for us: "we do not know how to pray as we ought" (Rom. 8:26). Even those of us who lead public prayer, who facilitate prayer groups, who write books on prayer! We do not know how to pray as we ought, "but that very Spirit intercedes with sighs too deep for words."

Invitation to reflect: How might the Spirit intercede in your prayers, in ways that are "too deep for words"?

We continue on the journey from slavery to freedom, from labor pains to new creation. Bondage, suffering, and decay are all around us, and yet there is going to be a new world, a Promised Land. It's true! "The sufferings of this present time are not worth comparing with the glory about to be revealed to us" (Rom. 8:18).

Intercession in Hebrews, James, and Revelation

Consequently he is able for all time to save those who approach God through him, since he always lives to make intercession for them.—Hebrews 7:25

Are any among you sick? They should call for the elders of the church and have them pray over them, anointing them with oil in the name of the Lord. The prayer of faith will save the sick, and the Lord will raise them up; and anyone who has committed sins will be forgiven. Therefore confess your sins to one another, and pray for one another, so that you may be healed. The prayer of the righteous is powerful and effective. —James 5:14-16

When he had taken the scroll, the four living creatures and the twenty-four elders fell before the Lamb, each holding a harp and golden bowls full of incense, which are the prayers of the saints.—Revelation 5:8

The later New Testament writings portray a rich understanding and practice of intercessory prayer. Building upon the memory of Jesus at prayer, and relying upon the teachings of the apostle Paul, whose letters often begin with intercession, these writings offer additional glimpses into how the early Christians prayed for one another. A few comments at the conclusion of this chapter will perhaps guide you into a deeper exploration.

In the letter to the Hebrews, Jesus is our great high priest (4:14), who has made the complete and perfect sacrifice for us. He is the mediator, the bridge between a Holy God and a sinful humanity. As high priest, Jesus makes intercessions for us (7:25). Through the prayers of Jesus, we have access to God. Thus Christians are not limited to the effectiveness of their own prayers or the worthiness of their own appeals. Thomas G. Long has written,

> When we approach God through [Christ], we find him to be a priest who can save completely and for all time (Heb. 7:25). We do not have a priest who gets sick and dies, or who goes on vacation, or falls down on the job, or grows tired of our need, or compromises his office, or takes advantage of us for his own gain; we have a faithful and steadfast great high priest who can be trusted, who "always lives to make intercession" for us (7:25).[1]

James advises the early Christians, and us, to see our sin, trouble, and sickness in a new way, as occasions for God's gifts—gifts of confession, intercession, and healing. James 5:16 reads, "confess your sins to one another." We are sinners. This is our human condition. Sometimes we sin against someone else, by what we say, what we think, or what we do. You and I share this in common. We are sinners. There is only one way out of sin, and that is confession. First John 1:9 says, "If we confess our sins, he who is faithful and just will forgive us our sins and cleanse us from all unrighteousness." Confession is naming the sin in the presence of someone you trust and then claiming the forgiveness as a reality.

The book of James describes a Christian community that practiced confession, intercession, and healing. All these practices were channels of God's mercy and grace, and strengthened the faith of individuals and the community of which they were a part.

In the practice of the early Christians, confession was closely tied to intercession, praying for others. If you have ever known that others are praying for you, you will appreciate how powerful that is.

Samuel, of the Old Testament, said, "God forbid that I should sin against the LORD in ceasing to pray for you" (1 Sam. 12:23, KJV). "Prayer is," in the words of Augustine, "to intercede for the well-being of others before God."

I recall a wonderful woman in a congregation I once served, who died a few years ago. Each time I visited her, as I prepared to leave, she would say, "I want you to know that I pray for you, and that I pray for the church every day." She could no longer be physically active or even present in the church. There were many things she could no longer do, but she could intercede. I would always say, "That is the very best thing you could do."

Where there is confession and intercession, an additional gift often emerges: healing. In modern times, healing has acquired a bad reputation as a result of hucksters who prey on the weak. Healing in front of television cameras seems completely foreign to healing performed by the One from Nazareth who would say, "Go in peace . . . your faith has made you well. . . . Don't tell anyone about this!" (See, for example, Mark 1:44 and Luke 8:48.)

The Revelation to John is a book about worship before the throne of God, who alone is worthy of adoration and praise. The golden bowls of incense are the prayers of the saints (Rev. 5:8), that is, the prayers of all of the Christians. These prayers are joined together with praise. In some ways the Revelation is a mystical and complex book, yet in other ways it describes a reality that we know and experience: we come into God's presence with singing (Ps. 100:2); we hallow God's name (The Lord's Prayer); we offer petitions and intercessions, sometimes sung, sometimes spoken. Our prayers rise like incense (Ps. 141:2) to the One who receives our worship. They acknowledge that "the kingdom of the world has become the kingdom of our Lord and of his Messiah, and he will reign forever and ever" (Rev. 11:15). Therefore we approach the throne of grace with confidence!

Invitation to reflect: What insights do you gain from reviewing these three later New Testament letters? How do their teachings affect your thinking or praying? Think back over your own experiences in prayer and identify any occasions when you were "in the spirit on the Lord's day" (Rev. 1:10).

Chapter Three

Intercession and Compassion

He had compassion for them, because they were like sheep without a shepherd.—Mark 6:34

The practice of intercession enlarges our sense of compassion. When people ask for prayers, they are saying something about God and about other people. The request is itself an act of trust, trust grounded in the hope that God is compassionate and that other people reflect the image of God.

What we hear shapes us. "Faith comes from what is heard," Paul wrote to the Romans (10:17). *To hear* is connected in its linguistic origin to *obedience*—audio, auditory, obedient. "Hear, O Israel," the Shema, the basic prayer of our ancestors the Jews, conveys the profound call to obey. We are shaped by the voices that we listen to. British theologian David F. Ford writes:

> That is how hearts are shaped—by the music of voices we make our own. . . . To ask "Who am I?" leads straight to the other people who are part of me. . . . An experienced psychotherapist told me that a great deal of his work has to do with the quality of the "community" that clients carry around inside them.
>
> How do we discover the shape of our hearts? . . . We can find out who are the leading members of our inner community. . . . It begins as an exercise in naming the most significant

others. . . . . We always live in their presence, whether they are physically there or not.[1]

We make room in our lives, in our hearts, in our brains for people who speak to us, for us, and about us. We are the sum total of all those voices.

INTERCESSION AS WILDERNESS

Prayer is a time to be quiet, to find a wilderness place, so that we might begin to hear those voices. The world will drown out these voices with elevator music. When we attend baseball and basketball games, we cannot carry on conversations amid the roar of music in the background; we can't hear the chatter or the plays being called. This is true in life as well.

The authors of the Bible know that we always find these quiet wilderness places and times to be a struggle, and yet the Promised Land presents its own dangers. In the Promised Land we are tempted to silence the voices, to crowd them out, to hear only the pleasing voices, and maybe even to press the mute button on the word of the Lord.

We have entered into the Promised Land, Moses writes; we have settled it, settled into it, harvested it, and enjoyed the fruit of it (for instructions on living in the wilderness, read Exod. 16 and Deut. 8). We have forgotten what the desert was like, have even forgotten that God's power and provision made the Promised Land possible. We have become rich and self-sufficient. And so, the Lord says, eat your meal with the Levites and with the aliens—not the aliens of *Star Trek* but the people who are in their own wildernesses now—the homeless, the stranger, the person who doesn't have it all figured out. Set a place for them, Moses says.

Set a place for strangers. Listen to their voices. This is the work of compassion. This is the practice of intercession. Congregations, at their best, make places for the stranger through compassionate, sometimes almost hidden ministries. Many faith communities make space for the homeless in winter, or for those struggling with addictions, or for immigrant families seeking to make a new life in a challenging environment. At our best, we set a place for strangers; we prepare a place for them. *Bless you,* God says, whenever we are compassionate, whenever we are hospitable. Because once we were in the wilderness. Our ancestors were there.

Invitation to reflect: If you are in a faith community, think about ways in which you make a place for the stranger. Where do you see other opportunities?

Strangers really are our own people. The strangers are in our own families. A friend who taught at a prestigious university for a good portion of his life was tenured, held an endowed chair, and received every teaching honor the school offered. But his faith and convictions led him to take a position at a school not ranked nearly as high in the national magazines; it was a school with a more distinctively Christian focus. He and his wife have an adult child who struggles with a medical condition that often leads to unpredictable and destructive behavior. Announcing his acceptance of the position at the new university would be an occasion for a public event at the school, so my friend met with the president and was honest. He told him about their son, that his son might do or say something outrageous; this was a part of their lives they attempted to manage but really could not control.

The president assured him that there was no problem. Later this father reflected on the school he had left: image and appearance had been so important there; his son had seemed like an embarrassment during his time there.

The church of Jesus Christ always makes room for the voices of those who struggle. In our prayers, as compassion is enlarged, we make space for those who struggle. For a few years I taught an occasional Bible study in a prison near the church I served. Often members of the church would go with me—to read the scripture, to offer music, to pray. Each time, after the experience, one of those people would write to let me know that a member of his or her own family was also in that very prison.

Invitation to reflect: How is wilderness a part of your own experience? Consider asking a trusted friend to pray for you in the wilderness places.

INTERCESSION AS HOSPITALITY

Do not neglect to show hospitality to strangers, for by doing
that some have entertained angels without knowing it.
—Hebrews 13:2

The fundamental basis for intercessory prayer lies in the basic human condition: we are all of us strangers, wounded in some way, living at some distance from the safety and sanctuary of home.

Deep, biblical intercession is a time to hear voices, all different kinds of voices: the voices of the poor, the confused, and the lost. These are people who don't quite belong in the Promised Land, but we meet them in the wilderness. While hearing voices in the wilderness is not always fun, it is at the heart of being God's people. The Hebrews wandered in the wilderness, being tested; Jesus spent forty days in the wilderness, being tested. If you are going to be a Christian, you are going to be tested. If you are going to be a Christian, you are going to hear different voices. Some will lead you down one path, some the opposite. Some of these voices are ones that we need to hear. In the hearing of those voices, and in the responding, we discover that we are being changed, even transformed.

Our prayer lives take the shape of a hospitable place. People inhabit our hearts. Some are known to us; some we will never meet. A hospitable heart is large enough to be patient with people, whatever their condition in life, and especially those different from us. A hospitable heart is the heart of God, the God who is gracious and merciful, slow to anger and abounding in steadfast love.

INTERCESSION AND THE PAIN OF OTHERS

My God, my God, why have you forsaken me?—Psalm 22:1; Mark 15:34

Congregations and the lives of those who gather in them form the context of intercession. At times the lessons are vivid, if one has eyes to see and ears to hear. One Holy Week brought a terrible accident to the congregation I was serving: the deaths of three beloved teenage boys. The deaths were devastating for their families, and by extension for their friends and for the church that would surround them in days ahead. The two families who lost sons were well known throughout the community, and the profound grief was known and experienced outside the church. As a pastor I encountered individuals, many of them parents also, who would make the connection with our church or with the families or with me, and then a comment would be made: "I don't even want to go there. I cannot imagine what that must be like."

Of course, neither they nor I could imagine the depth of suffering or the magnitude of loss felt by the grieving families. But I began to sense that these comments revealed a lack of engagement with the practice of intercessory prayer in its simplest expression, in the willingness to enter into the pain and suffering of another. Many of us act out of a flawed understanding of prayer, assuming that prayer facilitates avoidance of an issue, a person, a difficulty. But what if authentic intercession is the willingness to enter into the dark night of another, to stand beside a person, to carry his or her sorrows, to imagine the unimaginable? In this way, an intercessor carries out the work of Jesus on our behalf.

God not only imagines what a human life might be like but also takes human form (Phil. 2). God not only senses our grief but also bears our griefs and carries our sorrows (Isa. 53). God not only observes our mortality but also, in Jesus Christ, dies our death. The arms of the cross extend into the deepest human pain, experienced already in the one who voiced the words of the psalm, "My God, my God, why have you forsaken me?"

I am not judging those who commented about the daunting prospect of entering the pain occasioned by the death of a child. They were being honest. I am asking the question: what if intercession, practiced by Christians with and for one another, leads to a different response? What if we are called, out of compassion, to "go there"? What if we are invited—even required—to imagine what the pain of others might be like?

INTERCESSION: STRONG AT THE BROKEN PLACES

In 2011 we marked the tenth anniversary of the events of September 11, 2001. In a way 9/11 seems to be in the distant past, and in another it remains fresh in our memories. I will never forget the impact of that experience on our community. It had been an exhausting and painful week, a week of brokenness. We were all trying to make sense of the human tragedy in the days following 9/11. We all did so in our own ways: airline pilots and their families asked questions about security; financial analysts wondered about the economic implications; engineers thought about the devastation of structures; baseball fans wondered about having the World

Series in November. Of course, we all looked primarily at the human cost of all the destruction. It had been an exhausting and painful week, a week of brokenness.

I viewed the events and the reactions as a preacher, through the lens of the Bible. The previous week I had read from Jeremiah: "We look for peace, but find no good, for a time of healing, but there is terror instead" (Jer. 8:15). Now we were in a time of terror and destruction, a time of brokenness. That week we broke the bread, the Body of Christ, and we prayed in our own ways for a broken world, a world for which Christ died. The brokenness of our world was of course present in many ways beyond the World Trade Center and the Pentagon. Those were parables, signs of brokenness that we could see—repeatedly: the plane crashing into the 110-story building, a huge section of the fortress-like Pentagon reduced to rubble. We tried to make sense of those images.

Jeremiah was no different from us. He saw brokenness in his own time and place and tried to make sense of it. The potter's house in Jeremiah 18 was a vivid sign, one of the best for getting through to the people a message about brokenness. It reminded them of an important truth: we are strong in the broken places.

We are strong at the broken places because that is where God works with us. During the week of September 11, 2001, the broken places were obvious. We watched, over and over, as the plane flew into the building, as the building collapsed. But we also watched and perceived the work of God. We witnessed sacrifice and prayer. We observed people putting aside differences. We saw commerce stop and sporting events cease. Something of profound significance was occurring; this was decisive. We had observed the brokenness and known that God was there. The potter's house for us, in the week of 9/11, had been at the World Trade Center and the Pentagon. In subsequent years "the potter's house" would be seen in Abu Ghraib, in the aftermath of tsunamis, and in the wake of Hurricane Katrina.

Invitation to reflect: Read Jeremiah 18 and meditate on a broken place in our world. Offer a prayer on behalf of the brokenness, that there might be a new creation.

We all have our broken places. Yes, sometimes we hide, gloss over, and deny their existence. But for every one of us there is a broken place. And that is where God works with us. Henri J. M. Nouwen, in his simple and beautiful book *Life of the Beloved*, writes these words:

> Our brokenness reveals something about who we are. Our sufferings and pains are not simply bothersome interruptions of our lives; rather, they touch us in our uniqueness and our most intimate individuality.[2]

Every person is unique because he or she is created in the image of God. And every person is unique in his or her brokenness. And our brokenness is where God is at work in our lives.

We are strong at the broken places because God's strength becomes visible in our weakness. The clay in the potter's hand signifies that the potter is working, shaping, molding. God is the potter, and we are the clay. And through the events of our lives, God's strength is made visible in our weakness. During the 9/11 experience a group of passengers evidently learned of the destruction that would result from their hijacked destination. And so they fought the hijackers, at the cost of their own lives, to save the lives of many others.

"Do you see the sign?" Jeremiah would ask us. That God's strength is made visible in our weakness.

That same week a group of firefighters risked their lives to enter into a melting and collapsing inferno. Many of them died, we later learned. They did their work, what they were called and commissioned to do, at the cost of their own lives, to save the lives of others.

"Do you see the sign?" Jeremiah would ask us. That God's strength is made visible in our weakness.

It happened that a priest was among the firefighters at work in the World Trade Center on 9/11, administering last rites. Debris fell onto him, killing him. The firefighters, like pallbearers, carried his body to the nearest church. There they placed it on the altar. God's strength was made visible in our weakness.

We are strong at the broken places because we know that God is not finished with us yet. "Before I formed you in the womb I knew you," the Lord said to the prophet (Jer. 1:5). The word for "to form" in the Hebrew is the also the word for potter. In other words, God formed us, and God is still forming us. God created us, but God is not finished with us. I love this comment attributed to John Newton: "I'm not what I *ought* to be. I'm not what I *want* to be. But thank God, I'm not what I *used* to be!"

What is destroyed, the potter says, can be reused, recycled. We have been witnesses to destruction and devastation. Jeremiah points to signs, visual images. The visible signs are in our world, if we have eyes to see them. The brokenness of buildings, the abuse of children, the flooding of homes, the drowning of individuals, the torture of the innocent, the degradation of the earth. The broken places and the broken people teach us about the fragile quality of life and remind us not to take the people in our lives for granted. They also call us to compassionate intercession.

Jeremiah pointed to the sign of the potter's house. Another sign, for the Christian, is the sign of the cross. The cross stands above every other sign: race, nation, ethnicity, class. When American Christians pray, we remember that we are one nation under God, and for this reason that flag stands under the cross. We pray for our nation in its brokenness, knowing that we worship a God who blesses and a God who judges, a God who holds us accountable and a God who extends mercy.

In the midst of crises we keep these signs in our minds and hearts. The brokenness calls forth our prayers and our love, our gifts and our compassion. There are practical ways to respond to brokenness: donating blood; giving money to relief; getting on with our lives, making a difference where we are, doing something about the brokenness of our own city and region; welcoming the strangers who resemble the biblical refugees of which the Torah speaks.

The cross draws us deep into the heart of God. A broken world grieves a prophet like Jeremiah. A broken world grieves the heart of God. If you are a parent, maybe you have grieved when your child has endured an accident or an illness, a divorce or an addiction. When Jeremiah says he is sick with grief, you know what he means.

The God of the Bible grieves over the brokenness of the world. God is compassionate, and therefore God calls us to be compassionate. God sees the whole world, and the brokenness of the world, especially when brought on by radical evil, grieves the heart of God. The cross reminds us of that. The cross of Jesus Christ is the ultimate sign that we are strong in the broken places. To reflect on the world is to carry its burdens. These burdens, heavy with emotion, bring rising tides within many of us of almost palpable anger and grief.

> Because nothing can separate us from the love of God,
> > we are strong in the broken places.
> Because God is our refuge and strength,
> > we are strong in the broken places.
> In the name of Jesus Christ,
> > we are strong in the broken places.

Invitation to reflect: Recall a time when you experienced God's compassion. Give thanks. Consider the possibility that you might be the instrument of God's compassion in the broken places of our world. Discern a way to respond.

Chapter Four

Intercession and Community

Rejoice with those who rejoice, weep with those who weep.
—Romans 12:15

If one member suffers, all suffer together with it; if one member
is honored, all rejoice together with it.—1 Corinthians 12:26

Intercession helps us to discover the reality of the body of Christ.
As we pray for one another, the body of Christ, the church,
becomes visible to us. In the letters found in the New Testament,
Paul asks the churches to pray for him. In his letters, Paul develops
a vision of the church as an organic body, with gifted individuals,
different in their contributions and yet sharing a common life in
the Spirit.

In the letters to the Corinthians, Paul also reflects on the
meaning of human weakness and failure. As Christians, we will
experience seasons of weakness and of strength. We will know success and failure. Our lives mirror the rhythms of the liturgical year:
we wait, we hope, we anticipate; and then there is an answer, a fulfillment. We live in the chaos of wilderness; we experience loss, and
even death; and then there is resurrection and unexpected new life.

"Rejoice with those who rejoice," Paul writes, "weep with those
who weep." We are most fully the body of Christ when we allow

others to know our deepest joys and our darkest sorrows. Often our experiences with other Christians do not go beneath the surface. "How are you doing?" we are asked. "Fine, and you?"

We long to share what is really important to us. We need to let someone else know how it is with our souls. But we also wonder: *Will I be perceived as bragging if I let someone know that something wonderful is happening in my life?* Or *Will this person really care if I say what is weighing on me?*

We search for individuals within the body of Christ who can live into the admonition to rejoice with those who rejoice and weep with those who weep. These persons represent our most profound experience of Christian community. They are our intercessors.

Invitation to reflect: Make a short list of persons who would listen as you shared a deep joy or a dark sorrow.

We find these persons in the most common and unlikely places: Sunday school classes, choirs, sharing groups, committees, mission teams, the older woman who arrives early for worship and sits in the same pew each week. They are our intercessors. They are the body of Christ.

When I was a college student, I spent a wonderful summer working as a counselor in a Christian camp in the mountains of western North Carolina, about three hundred miles from my home. One evening I was playing in a basketball game. Our camp staff was competing with the staff of a nearby camp. Playing defense against a fast break, moving backward, I tried to get into position before the other player took his shot. As I moved backward, another player collided with me.

This is my last memory of the accident. I was taken for surgery to repair a shattered cheekbone at a nearby hospital. The recovery lasted several days. Thirty years later two memories stick with me: the presence of my family in the hospital and a letter from the small choir of my home church. I had developed friendships with several of the members of the choir in which I sang. The letter simply stated that they were remembering me in their prayers, and then each person had signed the card.

A simple gesture—yes. But nevertheless, a physical reminder that the body of Christ was real, and that I was a part of it.

EXERCISING THE BODY OF CHRIST

In the practice of intercession we become priests to and for one another. Clergy and laity often discover contexts for this form of prayer, which are, I am convinced, open windows to God's wind, or spirit. Intercession in the following contexts holds particular promise for the Spirit's movement:

- *The birth of a child.* Intercessory prayer is spoken on behalf of the parents (that they would be blessed with guidance, patience, strength, and wisdom) and the child (to grow up knowing his or her identity as a child of God and claiming the faith for himself or herself).

- *The conversion of an individual.* Intercession could focus on the gift of salvation and the hope that the new Christian would live into the fullness of God's grace through the practice of disciplines and participation in the body of Christ.

- *The welcoming of new persons/members of congregations.* A prayer of intercession would honor their search for community and ask God to guide them toward welcoming persons.

- *The call to a form of ministry or mission.* Intercessory prayer would ask for God's guidance, for the gifts and resources to fulfill the mission, and for the assurance that God promises to be with us (Matt. 28:19-20).

- *For pastors, leaders, and missionaries.* Intercession provides strength for those who lead God's people, individuals who often experience isolation, doubt, and conflict. The prayer might use the imagery of branches connected to the vine (John 15) and recall the strength we draw from our relationships with Christ and one another.

- *The visitation of the sick.* Prayer in this context would acknowledge that we provide care but not necessarily cure (a distinction at the heart of the Stephen Ministry) and would serve as a reminder to the one sick that we are never alone; God is with us.

- *The circle of grief.* Intercession acknowledges that there is more to life than our earthly pilgrimage and confesses our belief in life beyond death (John 11).

Here are other community contexts in which intercession can play a significant role.

- *Parenting and grandparenting.* Intercession takes the form of petition for safety, providence, faith, and love.

- *Spiritual friendship.* Prayers might be shared by friends who support each other, share deeply in an atmosphere of trust, and have known each other over a significant length of time.

- *Enemies.* In this distinctively Christian form of intercession, the petition includes a desire for reconciliation with those who have harmed us and those whom we have harmed. It expresses the conviction that the grace of Jesus Christ is both costly and amazing.

- *Devastation.* In crises that arise, intercession names the pain of a broken world, sometimes ravaged by natural phenomena, at other times by human action, and connects the pain of the world with the care, grace, and providence of God.

- *Peace.* In a violent world, followers of Jesus, the Prince of Peace, fulfill their calling to be peacemakers by praying for reconciliation and healing, and draw strength from the prophetic hope that the wolf will lie down with the lamb (Isa. 65).

OUR STRENGTHS AND WEAKNESSES

In intercession, we do for others what they cannot (or will not) do for themselves. In our moment of strength, we reach out to others in their moment of weakness. This is the beauty of a common life, shared by Christians, over time. "For everything there is a season," the writer of Ecclesiastes suggests, "a time to weep, and a time to laugh" (3:1, 4). The body of Christ functions when individual members share their strengths and weaknesses, when they rejoice and weep.

A recurring experience for pastors and leaders of congregations is the annual financial stewardship campaign. These campaigns bring out the best and the worst in people. They call forth our gifts, and they make visible our flaws. On several occasions I have had conversations with individuals who let me know that they would not be able to make financial contributions because of lost employment. Over time I have learned to respond in the following way: "You are a part of the body of Christ. In the past you were able to give when others were not in a position to do so. Now, in the present, someone else will contribute, because you are not able to give.

And in the future, the time will come when you will be able to give in a way that helps someone else, who is in a difficult place."

> I wonder whether you realize a deep, great fact. That souls—all human souls—are interconnected? . . . we cannot only pray for each other, but *suffer* for each other. . . . Nothing is more real than that interconnection—this gracious power put by God . . . into the very heart of our infirmities.[1]

We intercede with our gifts and with our prayers. In our moments of strength we intercede and pray for those in their own moments of weakness. We do something very important for someone else, something that is beyond human effort or strength.

Invitation to reflect: The story of a paralyzed man brought to Jesus by his friends is found in Luke 5:17-26. Read this passage and then imagine yourself in a time of weakness in your own life. Who are the friends carrying you? Or imagine someone near to you who needs the prayers of others. Bring that person in the presence of Jesus through your prayers.

ALL INTERCONNECTED

We are not isolated Christians. The New Testament was written to communities, new gatherings of Christians, who depended on one another in keeping this new faith alive. A prominent heresy in our time is that personal faith trumps everything else, that God speaks to the individual heart, that my own response to the gospel is all that matters. While the faith is personal, it is only so in relation to the historic faith, into which we are baptized, and the body of Christ—the church—in which we worship, study, pray, and serve. We are interconnected.

The book of Acts records the story of the first Christians. "They devoted themselves to the apostles' teaching and fellowship, to the breaking of bread and the *prayers*" (Acts 2:42, emphasis added).

The first Christians prayed for one another, in Temple worship and in their homes. It happens even now. We pray with a family, in a circle, hands joined, as someone has died or as a youth mission team returns home safely or as someone goes into surgery. Prayer partners stay in touch over the Internet. Men gather early in the morning to pray. We pray for missionaries across the planet. Individuals use *The Upper Room* devotional, either in magazine or e-mail form, as a guide to personal devotion. We take a day of prayer to remember the people of Sudan. We pray that distinctively Christian prayer, the prayer for our enemies (Matt. 5:44). We ask. We confess. We say thank-you. Christians are people who pray. Prayer is essential, as natural and as necessary as breathing. John Wesley wrote in a commentary on 1 Thessalonians 5:17 ("Pray without ceasing"): "Prayer may be said to be the breath of our spiritual life."[2]

Intercessory prayer disciplines us to remember this truth. The sorrow of someone else becomes my sorrow. The struggle of a friend weighs upon me. And the accomplishment of a friend helps me to see my own world in a brighter hue. Again, the image of the body is essential. I am not the body of Christ. I am a member of the body.

Within the body, pain sometimes exists. Within a local church, there may be conflict or even disillusionment. We may be tempted to flee, to approach God on our own. Yet we are a part of God's people, the body of Christ. Thomas Merton noted that "the love that unites us will bring us suffering by our very contact with one another, because this love is the resetting of a body of broken bones."[3]

To say that we are interconnected presents a challenge to us. Sometimes being interconnected is painful. But at other times it gives us great strength and comfort. We see this expressed in the latter portion of Hebrews 11. We can read these words, and in our imagination we see people we know, people who have lived with faithfulness, people who have been tested by suffering—"destitute, persecuted, tormented." *The Message* translates those words "homeless, friendless, powerless." And then a curious comment: all those, even in their faithfulness, "did not receive what was promised, since God had provided something better so that they would not, apart from us, be made perfect" (vv. 39-40).

We can comprehend that we need our ancestors who came before us. But the writer says that they need us! How do those who came before need us? Together, and with pilgrims across the centuries, we march in a processional to the throne of God's grace. This is Christ's body as a mystical communion.

> Therefore, since we are surrounded by so great a cloud of witnesses, let us also lay aside every weight and the sin that clings so closely, and let us run with perseverance the race that is set before us, looking to Jesus the pioneer and perfecter of our faith, who for the sake of the joy that was set before him endured the cross, disregarding its shame, and has taken his seat at the right hand of the throne of God.—Hebrews 12:1-2

These brief verses give a vivid picture of what it means to live as Christians. We are surrounded by a cloud of witnesses. We are not alone. John Wesley wrote, "I shall endeavor to show that Christianity is essentially a social religion, and that to turn it into a solitary religion is to destroy it."[4] We are not alone.

We celebrate the sacraments of Holy Communion and baptism within the church. In each we are reminded that we are not alone. In Communion we come to receive the bread and the cup, and we kneel alongside others; we kneel where others have knelt before us, and we know that we are not alone. In infant baptism we bring our child to the font and the water washes over the forehead. We claim the grace for this child and promise to surround this child with forgiveness and love. We know that we are not alone.

Sacraments are outward and visible signs of an inward and spiritual grace, that we are not alone. Maybe as you make your way through the week, it is easy to forget that truth. A few years ago I read an article in *Fortune* magazine titled "You Are Absolutely, Positively on Your Own." That essay on the workplace, outplacement, and downsizing is more relevant than ever. Perhaps you are working with difficult people, and the job never really seems to get accomplished, and you feel like you are on the ship all by yourself. It is easy to feel that you are alone.

This sense of isolation pervades our culture. In his book *Bowling Alone*, Robert Putnam observes that fewer people than ever are in bowling leagues, but more people than ever are bowling. Community in North American culture is collapsing. We are not reaching out to one another. It is easy to think that we are all alone and to live as if we are all alone.

The Hebrews were tempted to give up, to turn back, to fall away. No, says the writer. Look a little more closely. Since we are surrounded by a cloud of witnesses, we can lay aside every weight and sin. We can relinquish something. We can let go. We can surrender. We can shed some of the excess baggage.

It's not that *we have to do it*. We *can* do it. I am indebted to Ken Callahan for this insight, and for his reflection on this portion of Hebrews 12. We can release it. We can let it go, "it" being that which weighs upon us and keeps us from life-giving relationships with God and one another. In an article in the journal *Weavings*, writer Marilyn Chandler McEntyre describes a relationship with a woman who has much less formal education than she but has become a mentor to her. This woman has wisdom. And whenever Marilyn, a professor, confides in her older and wiser friend—whether anger, resentment, heartache—the friend has a saying, "Honey, you can afford to let that go."[5]

I like that: "You can afford to let that go." When I was a kid, revivals happened fairly frequently at our church; a recurring theme would be the state of our moral readiness if Jesus should come, if he should come today. I often wondered whether we would make it to the parking lot, or home for dinner, when the service ended, if the service ever ended. That's another story. But anyway, the question would be "If Jesus came to see you, what would you have to hide in your life, in your house, in your room?"

The writer of Hebrews approaches it a different way: We are surrounded by the cloud of witnesses—we are not alone—therefore we can lay aside every weight and sin: "we can afford to let it go."

Invitation to reflect: What in your life can you afford to let go? anger toward someone? some guilt within yourself? resentment toward a decision? a judgment about someone? dissatisfaction with the way your life is going?

Let us "lay aside every weight and sin," and "run with perseverance the race that is set before us." I went to the local YMCA early one evening recently, trying to maintain some semblance of health. When I arrived, two folks, all dressed up—T-shirts pressed, gym shorts that matched, nice running shoes—were leaning against the building, deep in conversation. I went in, ran my card under the scanner, found my machine, set it for thirty minutes. I can go about two and a half miles in that time. I finished reading what I had brought, drank some water, collected my keys, exited the door, and there they were, in the same place still, deep in conversation—the T-shirts, the gym shorts, the running shoes.

Let us run is the invitation in scripture. There is a time to select the correct clothing. There is a time to map out the race. There is a time to meet with a companion. But there is also surely a time to run. Let us run with perseverance the race that is set before us. In an invitation to hear God's call, Ken Callahan once reminded me:

some of us have been in the locker room long enough. It is time to run the race.

What does that mean? The time has come to put our faith into practice, to tackle something in life that seems to require more than we typically give. The time has come to stretch ourselves, to sweat a little. The time has come to share our faith with someone. The time has come to keep going, to break through the obstacle into our second wind, which is the Spirit's promise to carry us.

Do we stumble in the race? Do we fall behind? Are we tempted to quit? Yes. But we keep going. We think of the cloud of witnesses. "We feebly struggle," the hymn has it, "they in glory shine."

"Let us run with perseverance the race that is set before us, *looking to Jesus* (vv. 1-2, emphasis added). This is the important point—that we look to Jesus, trust in Jesus, follow Jesus, turn our eyes upon Jesus. Do you remember that cloud of witnesses? Imagine you are running the race, and the stands are filled with folks who are cheering you on, ecstatic that you are going to make it. They are intercessors for you. You are not alone. You have laid aside everything that weighed you down. You are going to make it because you are looking to Jesus. How do you look to Jesus? You read the Gospels. You say the Lord's Prayer. You stay close to his body, the church. You find him in the poor, the least, the last, the lost.

The life of intercession calls us to live faithfully before God. If in the practice of intercession we sense that we are alone—alone in our faith, alone in our struggles, alone in our convictions, recalling that "we are surrounded by a cloud of witnesses" carries us onward.

At times *we are weighed down*. We carry guilt and stress and sin; the baggage is too heavy for us. The invitation of scripture is life giving: "we can lay aside every weight and sin."

On other occasions *we are stuck*: we've been thinking about getting started, imagining ourselves farther down the road than we are, and we sense some urgency: "we can run the race that is set before us."

Or perhaps *we have been distracted*: life has been out of focus; we have trusted in false gods; we have chased too many dead ends. Remember the good news: "we can look to Jesus."

We are the body of Christ, the church; we do need one another. We are imperfect individuals, who come together to form an imperfect church. But God promises to do something with us if we stay together. A race, a journey, is before us: "We're marching to Zion, beautiful, beautiful Zion; we're marching upward to Zion, the beautiful city of God."

We are going to make it. We are going to make it *together*; we look to Jesus and discover that we are not alone but surrounded by a cloud of witnesses. We intercede for one another, discovering the good news that others are interceding for us. We are going to make it.

Chapter Five

Intercession and Mystery

Likewise the Spirit helps us in our weakness; for we do not
know how to pray as we ought, but that very Spirit intercedes
with sighs too deep for words.—Romans 8:26

PRAYER AND THE UNEXPLAINED

Intercession is a mystery. Yes, specific studies link meditation
with wellness, prayer with health, spiritual practice with physical functioning. Yet intercession remains a mystery. Some who
intercede have great clarity about what they are doing; others are
not so sure. Some who intercede discover a source of serenity; others feel troubled. Some sense that they are fulfilling God's purpose
in interceding for others; others wonder about any divine reality
associated with their concern.

Intercession is a mystery. In our culture we want definition,
which is also a way of controlling a situation. The idea that "prayer
doesn't change God, but prayer changes us" is an expression of this
attitude, because, of course, God is the mysterious agent in intercession. Prayer can never be reduced to the behavior modification
of people. Human transformation is the work of God, but God's
work is not limited to the changes that occur in us.

Intercession is a mystery. The transcendent God is called forth
to intervene in human nature and destiny. For this reason we cannot control the outcome of transcendence: it is storm, fire, wind,

flood, life out of and beyond death. We can only continue to be in prayer for others.

INTERCESSION AND SUFFERING

Sometimes it doesn't add up. "Life is good," the bumper sticker says, but sometimes life is *not* good. I probably don't need to give you chapter and verse. You can think globally—tsunamis in Southeast Asia, an earthquake in Haiti, HIV/AIDS in Africa, global warming in the Arctic north; or you can think locally—a coworker, someone in your neighborhood, or someone in your family or whatever challenge you may struggle with.

Invitation to reflect: Note a life situation that causes you to struggle as a Christian.

If you have lived for a time, you could probably write this chapter of the book. You could also, with the benefit of brief reflection, bear witness to the unfairness, the senselessness of it all; you could stand and shake your fist at someone, anyone, maybe even at God, and you could ask, even in a demanding tone of voice: *Why?*

Why? You would not be alone. Job, for one, would stand with you, alongside you (not to mention Jesus, who also asked, "Why have you forsaken me?"). Job would be there with you. We hear the phrase "the patience of Job," but as one of my professors pointed out, Job was patient for about two chapters. The book that bears his name has to do with this question *Why?*

Theologians have a name for this question: *theodicy.* The root word concerns God and justice, God and righteousness. *Theodicy* names the problem that sometimes things just don't add up, whether it is an AMBER alert or a Holocaust a generation ago or genocide today or the man born blind in John 9. How can we hold on to our faith in a loving and powerful God while living in a world where so much pain, suffering, torture, and inhumanity exist?

Even asking the question makes us a little uncomfortable. The church has never grappled well with this question; we have never given a privileged place to the book of Job. We want to be the church that swims in the cultural stream, a church "where seldom is heard a discouraging word." But there it is: Job, there in the Bible. Go to the Psalms and turn left. Forty-two chapters that dig deep into the exploration of one question.

Job does everything right, and then he is nailed. Everything he loves is taken away from him. Sometimes a person will come into my office expressing bewilderment: despite doing everything right, he or she has been overwhelmed in some way—an unforeseen event, a health crisis, a disappointment. Deeply faithful, deeply troubled.

We want to love and believe in God, and in the process we hope that it all adds up. Job knows where we are; he will stand with us.

His friends come alongside Job. They try to make it all add up, in some way. Do you know these friends? A child dies, and a friend comes along and says, "God needed an angel." A spouse dies, and a friend comes along and says, "You would not wish them more suffering." A terrible thing happens. People respond in compassionate ways, and a friend comes along and says, "It brings out the good in people." A layoff comes, someone is downsized, and a friend comes along and says, "It will make you stronger."

Invitation to reflect: How are our prayers, our prayer groups, our language about prayer sometimes unhelpful to others? Can you recall an experience when someone sought to offer comfort but instead caused greater pain or confusion for a person in need?

These friends are the descendants of Job's friends. Job's friends tell him that he should have a stronger faith, that he should not question (haven't you heard "It is not ours to ask why"?), that he must be at fault in some way. "God has a plan," they say. Embrace it. Get over it. Get on with it. *Where's the Job we used to know,* they wonder.

Here's the problem: Job's friends do not help him. They want closure, they want answers; they are as unsettled by the questions as we are. Oh, one other problem: they pretend to speak for God, but in the final analysis they are not truthful to God, at least not the God of the Bible. For thirty-five chapters or so, the friends of Job have their say, but then, mercifully, God intervenes. God speaks "out of the whirlwind." The NIV translates the beginning of chapter 38 this way: "Then the LORD spoke to Job out of the storm."

We have close friends who have lived through the storm. Dale and Kelly Clem were my classmates in divinity school. They were from Alabama, I was from Georgia, and so we shared a regional kinship. After graduation they returned to their home conference—Dale as a campus minister, Kelly as a pastor.

On Palm Sunday 1994, the congregation was worshiping at the eleven o'clock hour. In the midst of the service a tornado swept through Goshen, Alabama, devastating the Goshen United Methodist Church. Twenty members of the church were killed, including Dale and Kelly's four-year-old daughter, Hannah.

Dale and Kelly had experienced the fate of Job. Over the next days and weeks and months and years they would begin to put their lives together, to ask questions, to seek healing. Like Job, they would put aside the easy answers that just didn't seem to make sense. But like Job, they would also see God in the storm and know the reality of God in its aftermath.

In his journal, Dale described walking through the downed trees in their backyard in the days after the tornado and coming upon a little red wheelbarrow. He had left the wheelbarrow next to a storage building outside the house. The tornado had lifted the storage building and shifted it clockwise about two feet. The backyard was fenced in, but there was no longer a fence. A canoe was gone; a bicycle—who knows where it came from—was lodged in the trees. The tabletop of a metal garden table was missing, although the frame was still there. Dale imagined that it had flown away, like a Frisbee.

In the midst of all of this wreckage sat the little red wheelbarrow, exactly where Dale had left it. Dale had used it to carry debris in the backyard but mostly to give Hannah and her sister Sarah rides. Dale wrote:

> To me, that little red wheelbarrow represented endurance. It had survived the winds and chaos and was ready to scoop up and carry. The little red wheelbarrow became a symbol of faith. . . . our faith that endured the storm and our faith that will carry us through the dark days to come.[1]

Out of the whirlwind God speaks, the constant in the midst of change. What does God say? "Look at the world, Job. See the beauty as well as the tragedy, it is a dangerous world, but it is filled with grandeur and freedom; and, yes, it is filled with the unexplainable." To read chapters 38 through 41 is to be given a lesson in the awesome power and diversity of the world we live in. Who could have imagined it? Who can comprehend it?

Questions remain, but now the one asking the questions is God. Chapter 42, the last one of the book, marks a turning point. Job answers the Lord, "I know that you can do all things. I had heard of you, but now I see you. I repent in dust and ashes." Here Job is humble before God's majesty. It is enough for him to know that God is real. Like most of us, Job had suspected that clear answers probably were not likely, but he wanted to know God, to see God. "I had heard of you, but now I see you."

The Lord speaks again. The friends, who gave the easy answers, are criticized by God: "My wrath is kindled against you . . . for you have not spoken of me what is right, as my servant Job has" (42:7). Take these offerings, and go to Job, and "Job shall pray for you, for I will accept his prayer" (v. 8). They give the offering, and the passage concludes, "the LORD accepted Job's prayer."

But the story is not really over. One more truth will be discovered. After the suffering, after the experience of God's presence, what next? Job prays for his friends. They comfort him. God blesses Job. And one of the clearest signs of Job's renewal is his willingness to have more children, an insight I gleaned from Ellen Davis in her book *Getting Involved with God: Rediscovering the Old Testament*. Job is given ten children—seven sons, three daughters. He names the first daughter Jemimah, which means, in Hebrew, "dove," a reminder of God's sign of new life after the Flood.[2]

My close friends Blaine and Beverly lost both sons in an automobile accident. They journeyed toward the decision to adopt, and years later received a daughter from China. I am sure her life with them is a symbol of faith—like that little red wheelbarrow. God does renew the world; God does repair the creation.

Why do bad things happen to good people, like Job, like Dale and Kelly, like Beverly and Blaine? We ask that question for which, on this side of the mystery, there is no answer. It is enough to know that faithful men and women have walked this path before us; they have held their heads in their hands and screamed; they have wandered through the wreckage; and they have endured the pious explanations of their friends.

After the suffering, we listen for the voice of God, and we look for a sign: a wheelbarrow, a dove, a cross. The good news is that God always listens to us, God is always patient with us, God always speaks to us, out of the whirlwind. C. S. Lewis had it right: "God whispers to us in our pleasures but shouts in our pains."[3]

Finally, we are not given an answer by God; we are given the presence of God. "I had heard of you by the hearing of the ear," Job says, "but now my eye sees you" (Job 42:5).

INTERCESSION AND OUTCOMES

A part of the mystery has to do with unexplained suffering. Another aspect of the mystery relates to the anticipated outcomes and results for which we pray. Rowan Williams, archbishop of Canterbury, has defined intercession as "thinking of something or someone in the presence of God."[4] The practice of intercession aims to keep God and person, God and world, from falling apart. We belong together. This overarching goal offers a pathway into thinking about the intentions of our prayers. For a variety of reasons, we often pray for specific outcomes: we are asked to pray for health, that a program may be successful, that a home may be sold, that a person may find work. We often have our own ideas about happiness and success, about difficulty and pain. We want others to know the former and to avoid the latter!

This frame of reference can make intercessory prayer outcome-oriented and results-driven, and such a posture shapes much of the conversation about answered and unanswered prayer. Rowan Williams invites us to consider the simple bringing together of a person and God. In intercession, I might think not of my friend and his search for work but simply think of him in the presence of God: the light of God in all of its brilliance, the life of God in all of its abundance, the love of God in all of its mystery.

Such a prayer challenges us in a couple of respects. We can lose perspective and focus on one of the realities (God, the person) to the exclusion of the other. We can focus on the glory and majesty of God, but this is more appropriately praise and adoration; or we can see only the person in need and hear the request, but this is human relationship. Intercession holds both together: the person and God.

When our prayers focus primarily on thinking about a person

in the presence of God, we see the questions about outcomes in a different light. We trust the outcomes to God. We relinquish control. We pay attention, but our attention is less concerned with results. God is in control. We remember that God loves us and know that God has a purpose. When life seems chaotic and broken, God is in the midst of it—nothing can separate us from the love of God (Rom. 8:38-39). And so our most profound prayer is that God will stay close to God's people, even in the midst of the storms that rage and the wilderness that stretches as far as our eyes can see.

The scriptures tell the story again and again of individuals who sought to be faithful, even without knowing what the outcomes might be. Moses sees the Promised Land but does not enter it; Jesus says, "Not my will, but thy will be done." Abraham and Sarah go into a land that is unknown to them with only a promise. Esther risks her life to do what she knows is right. The eleventh chapter of Hebrews gives a panoramic glimpse of this reality: we seek to be faithful, we pray, but we cannot be sure about the outcome. While we do not know the future, we know the One who holds the future, the "Alpha and the Omega, the first and the last, the beginning and the end" (Rev. 22:13).

In our praying for others, we can let go of the outcomes that we desire. We can see the person, and think of her or him in the presence of God. This prayer will be sufficient, and God will be with us.

Invitation to reflect: Identify a concern in your prayer life that you would be willing to relinquish, trusting the outcome to God's will and providence.

PARTICIPATION IN THE INTERCESSION OF CHRIST

Christian prayer assumes not only the miraculous—that God speaks, listens, and responds through human beings—but also that God works in ways that are beyond our powers. Christian prayer also assumes that God is not bound by space or time. We are connected to our brothers and sisters in Christ across the planet (we celebrate this reality on World Communion Sunday) and with our brothers and sisters, fathers and mothers in the faith across the centuries (as we engage in the observance of All Saints Day, for instance).

These convictions about the scope and power of prayer are important for the one who intercedes on behalf of others, because the scriptures insist that in our devotion we join in a prayer that has already begun. The writer of Hebrews affirms that "he always lives to make intercession for them" (Heb. 7:25). Jesus is the high priest, the chief exemplar of intercession, and in our prayers for others we somehow participate, mysteriously, in his ongoing ministry.

Paul, writing to the Romans, reminds them that Jesus sits at the right hand of God and intercedes for us (Rom. 8:34). Thus our intercessions are not our own inventions nor our burden to be carried alone. We lift them up to the Lord. As we do, they are shaped, improved, revised, and gathered into the intercessions of all of God's people for one another and the world.

INTERCESSION AS COOPERATION WITH GOD

In intercessory prayer, we do not change the will of God. Or do we? There is a tradition in Old Testament prophecy in which the intercessor speaks to God and helps to restrain the divine anger at the people's unfaithfulness. But most of us wonder about this question because it implies that we know more about the human condition and destiny than God does. Even in our spiritual arrogance, most of us would like to avoid such a posture.

A positive meaning of changing the mind or will of God would be that we are partners with God in shaping the outcome. Maxie Dunnam's provocative question expresses this well: "What if there are some things God either cannot or will not do until people pray?"[5] Such a question calls forth our faithful persistence in prayer, and most of us are indeed motivated to pray because we have a desire for a particular outcome or result: a healing, a reconciliation, a response to grace.

The possible negative meaning is that we assume God to be at our disposal. We run through our list of requests, asking God for what we need. I am being blunt, of course, but in this case we are sending God on an errand to meet our needs and our perception of the needs of others. This egocentric form of spiritual practice causes some people to avoid intercession. Deep within, they know that a God worthy of worship will not be moved by such spiritual pride in which our intercessions are no more than wish fulfillment.

Humility can correct this negative practice. God's ways are not our ways, and we can acknowledge that God's will is sometimes revealed through providence and in God's own time. And yet the necessity of our active participation in intercession should not be lost. We are invited to cooperate in the work of God's grace. We are called into alignment in the unfolding will of God. At times we cannot be sure of the outcome, or of our effectiveness in prayer (note the parable of the good and bad figs in Jeremiah 24). We pray, entering into the mystery of the spiritual realm, seeing through a mirror dimly, yearning to see God face to face (1 Cor. 13:12).

INTERCESSION CHANGES US

Well-meaning persons may argue that prayer does not change God but does at times change the one who prays. There is truth in this statement but not the whole truth. Yes, we can be changed by prayer. Compassion replaces anger; empathy overcomes resentment. Our spiritual pride gives way to humility. As we pray, we are changed. But to leave it there would be to reduce prayer to a human experience, a psychological phenomenon. I am convinced that God is a full partner, an active agent in the prayers of Christians.

Something both human and divine is at stake. What this partnership means precisely defies description, but it is worth considering.

In prayer we have access to the transforming power of God that changes us and others in ways we cannot always anticipate. Prayer is more than the effect upon one who engages in the practice. Prayer releases an energy that is not present otherwise.

I was leaving a hospital, having visited a member of our congregation, and on the way to the parking lot I encountered a retired minister. He shared with me that the wife of a mutual friend, also a retired minister, lay near death in that hospital. He gave me her room number, and I reentered the building. When I stepped into the room I greeted my friend, his wife, and their pastor. We talked for a few minutes, and then the woman's pastor asked if we could pray together. He then invited another woman, an employee of the hospital, to join us in the circle of prayer. She gladly said yes and became a part of the prayer. As the five of us prayed, I sensed a release of God's energy in the room, a movement of the spirit, a synergy of grace. Like the best experiences of prayer, it was mysterious. And yet surely the presence of the Lord was in that place, on that afternoon.

Invitation to reflect: Reflect on intercession as the releasing of God's energy. How might such a spiritual practice make a difference in the life of a person in your family or congregation?

Chapter Six

Intercession and Practice

Jesus told them a parable about their need to pray always and not to lose heart.—Luke 18:1

On the first day after New Year's Day I went to the nearby YMCA to exercise. This was partly my discipline, partly my need, and partly my attempt to reverse some of the holiday damage. When I entered the facility I discovered that the place was packed! Lines had formed at almost every exercise machine. People bumped into one another on the crowded walking track. I had observed this scene in prior years, and realized, of course, that it was nothing new. We all desire to make a fresh start, maybe even to achieve an "extreme makeover"!

Fast-forwarding in my mind to later in the year, perhaps late March or early June, I could see that the facility would not be so crowded. I also knew that the persistence related to the practice of exercise would be difficult to sustain over the long haul. The spiritual lesson: we want to be transformed, we want a relationship with God, and yet most of us find it difficult to continue in the practice of prayer.

What can we say about prayer? Some of us pray. Some of us would like to pray more often than we do. Some of us would like to know what happens when we pray. We are all beginners at this, novices. "We do not know how to pray as we ought," Paul writes in his letter to the Romans (8:26). We don't know how to pray. More than 95 percent of people in our society believe in prayer, but do we really know how to pray?

THE PRAYERS OF JESUS FOR HIS DISCIPLES

One of the disciples speaks for us when he makes the request of Jesus: "Lord, teach us to pray" (Luke 11:1). Jesus first offers what we have come to know as the "Lord's Prayer." He teaches them a ritual. Rituals are valuable. In our family, if I began to ignore rituals—anniversaries, Mother's Day, birthdays—our family life would suffer. We need rituals in life, and that is true for prayer as well. If you have trouble praying, you might begin with the Lord's Prayer. Say the words, and listen for the phrase that seems to speak to you:

Thy will be done—placing our lives in God's hands

Give us this day our daily bread—trusting that God will provide

Forgive us our trespasses—claiming God's grace

As we forgive those who trespass against us—making the decision to be gracious to others

Lead us not into temptation—keeping us within God's purpose

"Teach us to pray," the disciples ask, and Jesus gives them these words. We have come to know them and love them, and because many of us say these words in worship, because they are a part of a ritual, we internalize them, and they become a part of who we are. When your prayer life becomes problematic or nonexistent, start by saying the Lord's Prayer as a point of reentry into the practice.

Invitation to reflect: Take a moment to say the words of the Lord's Prayer.

Jesus gives the disciples this ritual. Then, according to Luke, he tells a story about asking. The story, in part, deals with intercession. Of course prayer encompasses more than asking: prayer includes listening, waiting, confessing, giving thanks. But prayer is also asking. The more intense prayers in our own lives often have been occasions of asking God for something: for a healing; for a way out of a jam; for strength; for the ability to let go, to forgive someone else or to forgive ourselves; for some kind of intervention.

In Luke 11:5-13 Jesus encourages his disciples—and us—to ask: "Ask, and it will be given you; search, and you will find; knock, and the door will be opened for you." Jesus illustrates this directive to ask in the context of relationships we can easily understand: friendships and parents. In one story, we hear that if a friend pesters you about something for long enough, you'll give in; in the other, a question makes the point: if your child asks for a fish, would you give the child a snake?

The friend who pesters demonstrates persistence—sticking with it, not getting distracted, allowing the vision to lead and guide us. The Greek here means "keep on asking, keep on seeking, keep on knocking." You will receive; you will find; you will enter. That is persistence. And persistence is the key to answered prayer.

The second question has to do with what it means to be a parent. This is the more difficult one. Would a parent give a child a snake or a scorpion? The answer is yes; some would. Children have always been abused. But despite horrible examples of abuse and neglect, most of us flawed human beings will still give good gifts to our children. Jesus in essence asks, how much more will the Father give to you?

We don't know how to pray. What can we do? We begin in the awareness that we are invited to relationship with One whose nature it is to give. Simply becoming mindful of this connection encourages us in the practice of intercession.

DISCIPLINE AND PERSISTENCE

How do we respond to the invitation of Jesus? First, we can become more disciplined and persistent. A few chapters later, Jesus tells a parable to encourage his followers to "pray always and not to lose heart" (Luke 18:1). A widow keeps coming back to a judge with her request, and she finally wears him down; at last he gives in. I preached on this passage years ago, when my children were small, and I am quite convinced this is a part of the gospel they grasped immediately! Children know how to keep at it; they know how to wear us down, right? If you have been the recipient of the continuing requests of children, you will know what I mean.

If we are going to be in a relationship with someone, discipline and persistence will be required: hanging in there. A particular word out of the history of Christian spirituality helps here: *purgation.* We allow some things to be purged: our priorities, our egos, our need to be right, our need to be in control.

Invitation to reflect: Reflect on your own life and ask yourself, *What aspects of my life need to be purged?*

GOD IS GRACIOUS

Second, we can acknowledge God's grace. It is God's nature to give, to be generous, to forgive, to be reconciling. We access the gifts of God through prayer. We have noted Maxie Dunnam's provocative question: "What if there are some things God either cannot or will not do until people pray?" William Temple, the Anglican archbishop of a century ago, said, "When I pray, coincidences happen, and when I don't, they don't."

I experienced a rough adolescence for a number of reasons. Throughout high school and college I began to spend time with my grandmother, who lived nearby. I found myself going to her house for lunch nearly every day. This could have been due to the fact that she was an extraordinary cook. I can still taste her roast beef marinated in Coca-Cola from one of those classic small bottles. Something else drew me there, however, which I could not then name or articulate but now have the words to describe. In her home, in her presence, I experienced grace.

Prayer is spending time in the presence of grace. Why would we not be drawn to that on a regular basis? Perhaps you know these words by Charles Wesley:

> Jesus, thou art all compassion, pure unbounded love thou art;
> visit us with thy salvation; enter every trembling heart.[1]

Another significant word in the history of Christian spirituality helps here: *illumination.* Jesus loves us. Jesus wants to spend time with us. Jesus prepares a place for us. Realizing this causes the proverbial lightbulb to come on, and we see the reality of God in Jesus Christ. We believe in a God of grace.

GROWING IN LOVE FOR OTHERS

Third, because we are disciplined and persistent and because we believe in a God of grace, we can grow in love for one another. It is hard to dislike people we are praying for. Unfortunately, we find it easier to judge people than to pray for them. But I am convinced that the latter is more Christian, in the spirit of the Sermon on the Mount. We are not here to see through other people; we are here to see other people through. We grow in love for one another as we pray. The classic movement in the spiritual life takes us from *purgation* (giving ourselves to God) to *illumination* (recognizing that we are in the presence of grace) to *union* (the awareness that we are one in the spirit, that we are one in the Lord).

Prayer is about naming other people in the presence of grace, before God. When the body of Christ is filled with people who are disciplined in their prayers and who know God as "merciful and gracious, slow to anger, and abounding in steadfast love and faithfulness" (Exod. 34:6)—in other words, the God of the Bible—wonderful things occur. Miracles happen. Residual angers disappear. Petty disagreements are cast aside. Even real differences carry less importance because we see one another through a new lens.

Thomas Merton, one of my spiritual heroes, was born in France. As a young man, he enrolled at Columbia University in New York, and soon he emerged as a promising writer. A religious experience led him to enter a monastery in Kentucky, his home for the rest of his life. He chronicled his conversion in *The Seven Storey Mountain*, which became a best seller.

After a number of years in the monastery, Merton was allowed to travel to Louisville. Earlier in his spiritual journey Merton had been spiritually arrogant at times, seeing himself and the monks as superior to others in their commitments. In two of his books he described the experience in Louisville that changed his perception.

> In Louisville, at the corner of Fourth and Walnut, in the center of the shopping district, I was suddenly overwhelmed with the realization that I loved all those people, that they were mine and I theirs.[2]

> I seemed to have lost an eye for merely exterior detail and to have discovered, instead, a deep sense of respect and love and pity for the souls that such details never fully reveal. I went through the city, realizing for the first time in my life how good are all the people in the world and how much value they have in the sight of God.[3]

Disciplined persistence, experiencing grace, growing in love for others—these habits lie at the heart of the practice of intercession. Are you prepared to move more deeply into this practice? Maybe you have been functioning in your own strength, guided by your own wisdom, and something is missing. Maybe your body is out of breath. Maybe you are ready to say, with the disciples, *Lord, teach us to pray.*

Learning to pray may mean connecting once again with basic Christian practices, which include personal devotion and church ritual, the words of the Lord's Prayer or the text of a favorite hymn. Perhaps you can be reintroduced to an old friend, One who knows you and loves you and accepts you, wherever you are—"Jesus, thou art all compassion"—a God of grace. Or maybe you want to have more love for others than you do; less separation, more peace in this world and less division.

We confess that we do not know exactly how to pray. But if we are intentional about the practices of our faith, if we go to the place of grace, if we say the names of those who are in need before God, we will find ourselves on the way. Our sins will be purged. The light of God will shine upon us. A deep and profound union will weave us together. The breath, the Spirit of God, will fill us and raise us into a new life. And so we continue to ask, with confidence and boldness: *Lord, teach us to pray.*

THE FRIENDS OF INTERCESSION: PATIENCE AND HOPE

Patience and hope are human virtues, gifts of God. They create the atmosphere in which the practice of intercession lives and breathes. To intercede is to be patient, for outcomes are often uncertain and visible results difficult to see. To intercede is to be hopeful, for we are trusting in a vision that we do not yet grasp, journeying toward a destination that we do not yet inhabit.

Our culture values immediate experience and quick closure. We are accustomed to transitions that are completed efficiently, products that are created quickly, and packages that are shipped overnight. Many of us hurry much of the time. Patience, for these reasons, is countercultural.

Prayer best understood takes the long perspective and requires our patient perseverance. How do we become more patient? First, we remind ourselves that God is patient with us. A recurring refrain, found throughout the Old Testament, says this clearly:

The LORD is gracious and merciful,
> slow to anger and abounding in steadfast love.—Psalm 145:8

Invitation to reflect: Spend a few moments saying this verse of scripture, slowly. Focus on a word or a phrase that gets your attention. Repeat the word or phrase as an address to God; for example, "You are gracious." After a time of silence, imagine God speaking to you, saying the same words to you: "[your name] is gracious." Conclude with another period of silence.

When I think of individuals who have had the most positive influence in my journey, I notice that all have been patient: teachers, coaches, friends, coworkers, supervisors. When we are the recipients of patience, we know that we have received a wonderful gift. Patience is the friend of intercessory prayer. Without patience, intercession cannot do justice to the God who is gracious and merciful or to the person "standing in the need of prayer." Patience allows the divine will and purpose to unfold. When we are prone to premature closure, patience sees the possibility of a new creation (2 Cor. 5:17). Patience also makes a space for confession and repentance, reconciliation and a new covenant.

We may pray for individuals over the course of days, months, or years. When we do so, we pray patiently—steadfastly but patiently. We do not lose heart (Luke 18:1).

Invitation to reflect: Locate a copy of Augustine's *Confessions*. Read Book 6, Chapter 1, and Book 3, Chapters 11 and 12, which are Augustine's reflections on his mother's steadfast prayers to God on his behalf over many years.

Closely aligned to patience is the virtue of hope. Hope lifts our eyes above the present human condition and circumstance. Those who were patient with us saw us in hopeful ways: a student who might blossom; an athlete who might develop; a coworker who might contribute. Without hope, there is little motivation for patience. But where hope is present—and hope is a gift of God (1 Cor. 13:13)—there is a will to continue and a path forward. Walter Wink writes:

> *History belongs to the intercessors, who believe the future into being. . . .*
> Hope envisages its future and then acts as if that future is now irresistible. . . . There are fields of forces whose interactions are somewhat predictable. But *how* they will interact is not. Even a small number of people, firmly committed to the new inevitability on which they have fixed their imaginations, can decisively affect the shape the future takes.[4]

How can individuals keep persons close to them on prayer lists for months, years, even decades? The answer lies in the gift of hope. We hope for what we do not see, the writer of Hebrews confesses. We hope for changed lives, for healing, for provision of resources, for a new heaven and a new earth.

Each Advent our congregation lights the candles of peace, hope, joy, love, and light. Each Advent I preach a sermon that touches on the gift of hope. At times I will look back over sermons preached in prior years—I do not want to repeat myself! I note that the world was troubled—warfare, famine, terrorism, poverty. And yet we light the candle of hope anyway, for the prophets taught us to live hopefully, toward the vision of a new heaven and a new earth (Isa. 65:17).

Patience and hope are the friends of intercession. They prod us to stay with it; their presence encourages us not to give up or lose heart. Like friends, they are there when we need them most, helping us to walk in the right paths, lifting our hearts and spirits.

THE ENEMIES OF INTERCESSION: APATHY AND DESPAIR

Apathy and despair afflict all of us at times along the journey. If patience and hope are the friends of intercession, apathy and despair are its enemies. Life, for most of us, includes relationships with friends and with enemies. We learn to understand and live with them, hopeful for more of the former than the latter. But at times we will find ourselves in the company of apathy and despair. It will help us to get to know them a little better.

Apathy is characterized by a lack of compassion or care for others. At times our apathy is conscious, and at other times unconscious. We may not see the needs of others, or we may see them without sensing a desire to respond to them. We may have little energy for such a response; and the causes may be biological, psychological, or spiritual.

The apathy may be deeply rooted in our human sin, defined by the reformers as "the heart curved in upon itself." The heart curved in on itself is not oriented toward the needs of others. We may have a distorted vision (literally an astigmatism) about who we are in relation to others. We may see ourselves at the center, and our own needs may overwhelm any possibility of considering those of others.

Some spiritual writers suggest that the primary obstacle to intercession is not intellectual (questions related to God's power or will, or human participation in the effects of prayer) but relational. It might be true that we think (rationalize) our way out of relationships with persons whose situations cry out for God's intervention.

Despair is rooted in a loss of hope. We see people who are at the point of despair in scripture—Israel, despondent on the long and winding journey to the Promised Land, which seems like an illusion; the disciples, devastated on the way home following the death of Jesus, amid confusion as they walk on the road to Emmaus. Where there is no hope, we find ourselves in the grip of despair, which can have the feel of emptiness, betrayal, confusion, or doubt.

Despair often derives from a lack of vision for the future. When we are unsure about our destination, our motivation for moving forward begins to wane. Waning motivation can bring on fatigue, as the energy that propels us toward a goal is absent.

Despair is an enemy of intercession because a lack of confidence in God's ability to transform human lives dimishes our capacity to intercede. If we have no faith in God's desire to bless those in need, it will be easy to avoid praying for them. If we believe that human nature cannot change, prayers of faith are of little importance. And if we cannot conceive of the possibility that God can accomplish the miraculous—more than we can ask or imagine, as the letter to the Ephesians says (3:20)—our prayers are best left unspoken.

Despair comes to us through disturbing experiences, trying circumstances, or significant obstacles. Despair finds a person worn down and wearied. Apathy and despair are the enemies of intercession in that they prevent progress in this Christian practice: over time, they deplete our faith and assurance in the power of God to be present with us and for us. The good news is that hope and patience are precisely the gifts and virtues needed to overcome apathy and despair. The serious and sustained practice of intercession will be carried out amid apathy, despair, patience, and hope. With God's help, patience and hope allow us to maintain the practice, which, in turn—in the words of Jesus—enables us not to "lose heart."

INTERCESSION AS A SPIRITUAL PRACTICE

Intercession is a *practice* because it contributes to a way of life for a Christian that is

- biblically grounded,
- rooted in the Christian community,
- an expression of compassion, and
- aware of the mystery at the heart of prayer.

The latter two qualities, compassion and mystery, speak to two frequent arguments against intercession. Some do question the purpose of intercession in light of the need for moral action in response to human need; we need not regard this as a matter of choosing between the two. Intercession, grounded in human compassion, can lead us into more faithful action, and often does.

For those who question the intellectual basis for intercessory prayer, wondering why we would need to ask a gracious God for help or inform a wise God of needs, I have noted the mystery at the core of this practice. We are invited, even commanded, to pray for others, in the knowledge that we participate in some mysterious way in the work of God in healing individuals and relationships and in the repair of the world.

A *practice* is a habit that develops over time. Intercession as a practice in particular needs to be grounded in the scriptures. If our prayers are not biblical, we can soon find ourselves projecting our wishes onto others, demanding our way, impatient with the progress that is often difficult to perceive. If we do not offer our prayers in the context of a Christian community, we can feel isolated, easily discouraged, and disconnected from the gifts and strengths of the body. Scripture and tradition are the resources that shape the practice of intercession.

Invitation to reflect: Glance again at the chapters on intercession in the Old and New Testaments. Which examples—Moses, Jesus, the prophets, Paul—are most relevant to you personally?

Intercession can shape a way of life for the Christian to participate in God's work of intercession. This way of life, Dorothy Bass and Craig Dykstra have suggested, "becomes visible as ordinary people search together for specific ways of taking part in the practice of God, as they faithfully perceive it in the complicated places where they really live. It is like a tree whose branches reach out toward the future, even when the earth is shaking, because it is nourished by living water."[5]

For many Christians, intercession becomes a way of life. Most congregations have formal or informal networks through which the faithful pray for one another. Ordinary people offer these prayers as a way of searching together for a practice or discipline that holds God and persons in need together, often in "the complicated places where they really live."

We take part in the practice of God—the way in which God acts in relation to Israel, to the church, and at the same time gives life to us each day. We pray incrementally each day for the needs of that day. We take part in the practice of God who blesses the covenants of marriage and parenting, who leads us providentially into friendships and vocations. We pray situationally for the needs of those closest to us. If we keep a prayer list, we often find ourselves naming specific persons and concerns, working through them in prayer and staying with those that carry weight for us.

Invitation to reflect: God, a living reality and presence, is engaged with us, with others, and with the Creation. The pattern of this engagement is "the practice of God." How do you most often sense that God is present to us? How do you most often perceive that you are present to God?

The practices are related to the complicated places where people really live. In families we experience fear and loss of control, brokenness and conflict, but also happiness and blessing. In friendships we acknowledge sadness and sorrow but also joy and laughter. In our vocational lives we know confusion and frustration but also fulfillment and gratitude. Over time the practices stretch us to pray for the world, where we see the largeness of God and the wideness of God's mercy, and for our enemies, who are both a challenge to us and, at times, a critique of our spiritual lives.

Invitation to reflect: Take a moment to compose a list for your own personal use of persons and situations that fall into these categories: family, friendship, vocation, world, enemies.

Intercession is one of the most basic and universal of Christian practices. It goes against the grain of liberalism (we can do it on our own) and fundamentalism (everything works out for the righteous). It is sometimes spontaneous, but it is better understood as a practice that contributes over time to a way of life. Intercession can transform the person who prays, as well as the person who is the beneficiary of prayer. This transformation is a gift of God—Father, Son, and Holy Spirit—who created us, who lives and prays for us, who intercedes in ways that are beyond the comprehension of our minds or the adequacy of our words.

Two models of intercession—one personal, one congregational—are offered at the end of this book. Now that you have reflected on this essential Christian practice, I invite you to undertake it for the sake of others.

I pray that your own intercession will draw deeply from the living waters of a gracious and merciful God, that these prayers would take the visible form of branches flowering in the world, bearing fruit in lives that are being healed and restored, even when the earth is shaking.

Do Not Lose Heart

One of the influential congregations in the United States over the past several decades has been the Church of The Saviour in Washington, D.C., cofounded by Gordon and Mary Cosby and chronicled in a number of books by Elizabeth O'Connor. A guiding principle of this church is the necessity of an *inward journey* and an *outward journey*. The Church of the Saviour seeks to lead individuals into both prayer and service, carrying on the traditional Christian rhythms of action and contemplation.

These two callings—the inward and the outward journey—are sometimes held in tension in the life of a Christian. Most of us have a natural preference for one or the other, perhaps related to our inclination toward introversion or extroversion, but much more is happening here than psychological categories can describe. To follow Jesus is to find the lonely place of prayer (Mark 1) but also to encounter the centurion's servant (Matt. 8), the widow's son (Luke 7), and the man who was born blind (John 9). Jesus embodies a rich interior life of prayer, and he practices a correspondingly profound life of service to others.

Our intention to live an authentic spiritual life creates a tension as we seek to respond to human need. Should we act or should we pray? Is prayer a way of avoiding the situation or the path into a deeper participation in it? Are these useful distinctions? Must it be either/or? It is possible to hold together the inward and the outward journeys, action and contemplation. Someone has suggested that a spirit without a body is a ghost, while a body without a spirit is a corpse, a vivid image. Intercessory prayer without human response is unreal, immaterial. And action without intercession can be programmatic and lifeless.

Held in tension, intercession and service enrich each other. By interceding we may be led to the best course of action, the most appropriate gesture. By interceding we are more likely to be attentive to the person before us who needs our help. And then the action completes the prayer. A friend often comments that the answers to prayer are often within our hands.

A young man once found his way to our church looking for financial assistance. He and I sat in chairs across from each other. His presence interrupted that day for me, and my mind unfortunately strayed somewhere else—the sermon, a church meeting, a newsletter deadline. I asked about his specific situation, but I did not offer to pray with him. He gave me the details, and we worked out a plan; but it was a mere transaction. My action did not flow from prayer or contemplation, although I am sure God was present in spite of my inattentiveness and lack of compassion.

On other occasions, I have taken a deep breath, looked into the eyes of the person before me, and asked his or her name. Then, praying together, we asked for God's presence and for solutions to problems known and unknown to us. I have listened, and in those moments I have known the wholeness of intercession and service.

So what will you do with the ordinary and yet profound request, voiced by friend or stranger, with a quiet intensity or a pronounced urgency: "Pray for me"? How will you begin to pray, and how will your response become one that is faithful? How can your intercession become a practice filled with patience and hope?

Imagine that you have been in the presence of a holy and compassionate God. You have offered gifts of worship and silence, listening and humility, adoration and repentance. You have placed these gifts upon the altar, and there you have gazed upon the greatest act of intercession, the cross of Jesus Christ. You remember that Jesus continues to pray for you. He is the great high priest, seated at the right hand of God.

Now you are preparing to depart, to go forth into the world, to be the visible sign of the cross in the world—to pray, on behalf of a broken world, in the name of Jesus. As you enter more deeply into the practice of intercession, your engagement with those nearest to you and those seemingly farthest away, becomes over time a *cruciform life*. As you take up the cross, Jesus promises to be with you, his prayers joined to yours, his body present to nourish you, his blood to save you, his suffering to heal you, his words to guide you. Led by the light, the Word, and the Cross, you remember the command and promise of Jesus: Pray always. Do not lose heart.

Two Models for Intercessory Prayer

Dietrich Bonhoeffer wrote in his book *Life Together*:

> Intercession is not general and vague, but very concrete: a matter of definite persons and definite difficulties and therefore definite requests. The more definite my intercession becomes, the more promising it is.[1]

Two models for intercession are presented here. The first model is designed for an individual's practice, and the second is designed for members of a faith community to pursue collectively. The models assume that simplicity is a virtue and that we begin best as intercessors by praying for a few persons, those within our family and vocational callings.

A PERSONAL MODEL
SEVEN DAYS OF INTERCESSION

PRAY ON SUNDAY for the church, the pastor(s) and staff, and Sunday school teachers.

PRAY ON MONDAY for your work in the world, for those who are seeking employment or struggling with vocational decisions.

PRAY ON TUESDAY for your family.

PRAY ON WEDNESDAY for your friends.

PRAY ON THURSDAY for emerging needs in the world. Clip newspaper articles or save Web links to stories throughout the week and reflect on them in your prayers on this day.

PRAY ON FRIDAY for your enemies (recall the prayer of Jesus on Good Friday: "Father, forgive them").

PRAY ON SATURDAY for people in your life with special needs or challenges.

A CONGREGATIONAL MODEL
FORTY DAYS OF PRAYER FOR FIVE PERSONS

In this model, all members of a faith community are invited to choose five persons for whom they will pray over a forty-day period. This model works well during the season of Lent, but it can be used at any time.

1. A person in my family who needs God's grace the most.
2. A person for whom I am grateful.
3. A person with whom I have conflict.
4. A person who has a material need: work, housing, food.
5. A person who needs to know Jesus Christ as Lord and Savior.

Following are brief reflections on each of these prayers. I am grateful to three congregations who have participated in these "Forty Days" prayer disciplines I developed: St. Timothy's United Methodist Church, Greensboro, North Carolina; Mt. Tabor United Methodist Church, Winston-Salem, North Carolina; and Providence United Methodist Church, Charlotte, North Carolina.

WEEK 1: READ LUKE 15:11-32.

This week I am praying for a person in my family who needs God's grace the most. Our human nature leads us to be critical of those who are closest to us (see Luke 15). Living with other people gives us direct exposure to their shortcomings, weaknesses, and faults. And those who live with us have direct access to ours as well!

When you pray for a person in your family who needs God's grace the most, you move from an attitude of *judgment* to one of *acceptance*. You bear witness to God's love. You become a channel of God's grace and grow the fruit of God's Spirit (Gal. 5:22-23). God is patient with us. God invites us to be patient with one another, especially those closest to us.

Prayer may or may not change the mind of God, but authentic prayer always changes us. Consider those closest to you in this life's journey: the members of your immediate family. Choose one person who needs God's grace the most. Remember this person by name each day this week. See the individual through the lens of the waiting parent who sees the child a long distance away, reaches out to embrace, and welcomes the child home.

Reflections:

WEEK 2: READ PHILIPPIANS 1:1-11.

This week I remember a person for whom I am grateful, living or dead, a family member or a friend. None of us is self-sufficient. We depend on other people. Their gifts enrich us. We are sustained by the sacrifices of others. In remembering and praying for this person, may I realize anew how I am blessed.

As you pray, you may discover that you are one for whom another is grateful; the scripture teaches that we are *blessed to be a blessing* (see Gen. 12:3). Close your eyes and call to mind a person for whom you are grateful. Give thanks to God for that person by name. Conclude by reading Philippians 1:1-11 again.

Reflections:

WEEK 3: READ MATTHEW 5:38-48.

This week I am in prayer for a person with whom I have conflict. As I pray for this person, I remember that Jesus lived in conflict with many people. I also remember his example: he prayed for his enemies as he was being crucified (Luke 23:34), and he taught his disciples to love and pray for their enemies (Matt. 5:44).

We all tend to avoid conflict. Jesus encountered persons with whom he had conflict by praying for them. In this way he met them in strength and not in weakness.

As you pray for a person with whom you have conflict, you become a stronger person. When you pray for a person with whom you have conflict, you reach out in love rather than act in retaliation. When you pray for a person with whom you have conflict, you are becoming more like Jesus.

Reflections:

WEEK 4: READ JAMES 2:14-17.

This week I will pray for a person who has a material need. Each of us has spiritual needs, but we also have material needs. As I pray for the material needs of one person, I am remembering that God loves the world (John 3:16), that God entered the material world (1 John 4:2), that Jesus healed the physical body (Mark 5), that the human body is a temple of the Holy Spirit (1 Cor. 3). My belief that God provides for all of our needs, material and spiritual, is at the heart of my faith when I pray for a person with a material need.

Jesus was God's word *"made flesh"* (John 1:14, KJV). He was also a healer. He fed people (Matt. 14:13-21). He was concerned with the needs of the spirit *and* the body.

Your prayer might be offered for a person seeking employment, for someone spending the night in a homeless shelter, for a friend undergoing physical rehabilitation, for someone who is hungry, or for someone seeking medical care in Haiti.

Prayer may lead you to be a part of God's response in a tangible way. Intercession is always linked to action.

Reflections:

WEEK 5: READ JOHN 17:1-8.

I am praying for a person who needs to know Jesus Christ. I am praying that one person will come to know and follow Jesus Christ. I do so not out of a sense of spiritual superiority, as if I am better than the person for whom I am praying. I ask that God will somehow use me to reveal the love and grace of Jesus to one person. When I pray for a person who needs to know Jesus Christ, I am sharing a wonderful gift with someone else.

Consider a next step: invite this person to experience worship with you where the gospel will be communicated in powerful ways, in words and through music. This invitation can be an extension of your prayer, a means by which God is answering your prayer.

Reflections:

For Further Reading and Reflection

This brief volume is an introduction to intercessory prayer. If you want to explore this practice through additional reading, here are some works I commend:

Karl Barth, *Prayer*, ed. Don E. Saliers, trans. Sara F. Terrien, 50th anniversary edition. Louisville, KY: Westminster John Knox, 2002.

Kennon L. Callahan, *Twelve Keys for Living: Possibilities for a Whole, Healthy Life*, especially the chapter "Compassion." San Francisco: Jossey-Bass, 1998.

N. Gordon Cosby, "Intercessory Prayer," in *By Grace Transformed: Christianity for a New Millennium*. New York: Crossroad, 1999.

Maxie Dunnam, *The Workbook of Intercessory Prayer*. Nashville, TN: Upper Room, 1979.

John Koenig, *Rediscovering New Testament Prayer: Boldness and Blessing in the Name of Jesus*. Harrisburg, PA: Morehouse, 1998.

J. Ramsey Michaels, "Finding Yourself an Intercessor: New Testament Prayer from Hebrews to Jude," *Into God's Presence: Prayer in the New Testament*, edited by Richard N. Longenecker. Grand Rapids, MI: Wm. B. Eerdmans, 2002.

Yochanan Muffs, "Who Will Stand in the Breach? A Study of Prophetic Intercession," *Love and Joy: Law, Language, and Religion in Ancient Israel.* Cambridge, MA: Harvard University Press, 1995.

Douglas V. Steere, "Intercession: Caring for Souls," *Weavings* 4, no. 2 (March/April, 1989).

Rowan Williams, "Intercessory Prayer," in *A Ray of Darkness: Sermons and Reflections.* Cambridge, MA: Cowley, 1995.

Notes

CHAPTER ONE

1. H. Stephen Shoemaker, *GodStories: New Narratives from Sacred Texts* (Valley Forge, PA: Judson Press, 1998), 84.

2. Eugene H. Peterson, *The Message Remix: The Bible in Contemporary Language* (Colorado Springs, CO: NavPress, 2003, 1974), 1194.

3. C. S. Lewis, *The Screwtape Letters* (New York: Touchstone, 1996), 37.

4. Ibid.

5. Augustine, *Confessions*, trans. Henry Chadwick (Oxford: Oxford University Press, 1998), bk. 1, ch. 1.

6. David F. Ford, *The Shape of Living: Spiritual Directions for Everyday Life* (Grand Rapids, MI: Baker Books, 1997), 56.

CHAPTER TWO

1. Thomas G. Long, *Interpretation: Hebrews* (Louisville, KY: John Knox Press, 1997), 88.

CHAPTER THREE

1. David F. Ford, *The Shape of Living: Spiritual Directions for Everyday Life* (Grand Rapids, MI: Baker Books, 1997), 31, 32.

2. Henri J. M. Nouwen, *Life of the Beloved: Spiritual Living in a Secular World* (New York: Crossroad, 1992), 71.

CHAPTER FOUR

1. Friedrich von Hügel, *Letters to a Niece*, reprint of 1928 edition (Vancouver, B.C.: Regent College Publishing, 1998), 19.

2. http://www.christnotes.org/commentary.php?com=wes&b=52&c=5. Accessed 5/18/2011.

3. Thomas Merton, *Seeds of Contemplation* (New York: Dell, 1949), 48.

4. Quoted in W. Stephen Gunter, comp., *The Quotable Mr. Wesley* (Atlanta: Candler School of Theology, 1999), 56.

5. Marilyn Chandler McEntyre, "A Gentle Word," *Weavings* 19, no. 4 (July/August 2004): 26.

CHAPTER FIVE

1. Dale Clem, *Winds of Fury, Circles of Grace: Life After the Palm Sunday Tornadoes* (Nashville, TN: Abingdon Press, 1997), 56.

2. Ellen Davis, *Getting Involved with God: Rediscovering the Old Testament* (Cambridge, MA: Cowley Publications, 2001), 171.

3. C. S. Lewis, *The Problem of Pain* (New York: Macmillan Publishing, 1962), 93.

4. Rowan Williams, *A Ray of Darkness: Sermons and Reflections* (Cambridge, MA: Cowley Publications, 1995), 117.

5. Maxie Dunnam, *The Workbook of Intercessory Prayer* (Nashville, TN: Upper Room Books, 1979), 15.

CHAPTER SIX

1. "Love Divine, All Loves Excelling," *The United Methodist Hymnal* (Nashville, TN: The United Methodist Publishing House, 1989), #384.

2. Thomas Merton, *Conjectures of a Guilty Bystander* (Garden City, NY: Doubleday, 1966), 140.

3. Thomas Merton, *The Sign of Jonas* (Orlando, FL: Harvest/ Harcourt, 1981), 92.

4. Walter Wink, *Engaging the Powers: Discernment and Resistance in a World of Domination* (Minneapolis, MN: Fortress Press, 1992), 299.

5. Dorothy C. Bass and Craig Dykstra, "Growing in the Practices of Faith," in *Practicing Our Faith: A Way of Life for a Searching People*, ed. Dorothy C. Bass (San Francisco: Jossey-Bass, 1997), 203.

TWO MODELS FOR INTERCESSORY PRAYER

1. Dietrich Bonhoeffer, *Life Together* (New York: Harper and Row, 1954), 87.

About the Author

KENNETH H. CARTER JR. is a district super-
intendent in the Western North Carolina
Conference of the United Methodist Church.
His geographical area includes sixty-nine congregations in the seven westernmost counties
of North Carolina. He lives with his wife,
Pam, at Lake Junaluska.

Ken previously served as a pastor of congregations in East Bend, Greensboro, Winston-
Salem, and Charlotte, North Carolina, most
recently as senior pastor of Providence United Methodist Church.
He has preached on Day One/The Protestant Hour; at Duke University Chapel, Marsh Chapel of Boston University, and The Upper
Room Chapel, as well as in churches ranging from small mountain
parishes to churches with more than five thousand members.

Ken is a graduate of Duke Divinity School, University of Virginia,
and Princeton Theological Seminary. He was awarded an honorary
doctorate from the United Methodist University of Liberia.